# GAINING GROUND

## A BLUEPRINT FOR COMMUNITY-BASED
## INTERNATIONAL DEVELOPMENT

### Joan Velásquez

Co-Founder of Mano a Mano

*We're making a difference together.*
*Best wishes. Joan*

ISBN 13: 978-1-59298-939-3

Library of Congress Catalog Number: 2014904109

Printed in the United States of America

First Printing: 2014

17 16 15 14  5 4 3 2 1

Cover and interior design by Laura Drew

Beaver's Pond Press
7108 Ohms Lane
Edina, MN 55439–2129
952-829-8818

To order, visit www.BeaversPondBooks.com
or call 1-800-901-3480. Reseller discounts available.

DEDICATION

TO OUR PARENTS, WHO TAUGHT US BY EXAMPLE
THAT WE ARE OUR BROTHER'S KEEPER

EPIFANIO VELÁSQUEZ AND INES UREY
ARNOLD AND STELLA SWANSON

Partnerships are formed by a handshake—hand to hand. With these partnerships, Mano a Mano (Spanish for "hand to hand") has created an organization that touches the lives of thousands of Bolivians. Mano a Mano projects have transformed rural communities and helped Bolivian families not only survive, but thrive. *Gaining Ground* describes the many achievements of this vital organization.

While visiting one of the medical clinics we helped dedicate in Bolivia, we experienced the immense gratitude of the rural community. Many people walked hours to attend the opening of the clinic. It was a highly emotional and moving experience that clearly demonstrated the significance and impact of Mano a Mano. What a different world we would have if our country's global outreach emulated the powerful community-based model of Mano a Mano.

—DAVID H. OLSON, PH.D. & KAREN OLSON
CO-FOUNDERS, PREPARE/ENRICH

Mano a Mano does not work "on" underserved Bolivian communities; it works "with" them. And this makes all of the difference. It engages local government and community leaders, health-care providers, educators, and ordinary citizens in a manner that taps local strengths and resources as all participants work together to realize this mission.

*Gaining Ground* documents the journey of its founders, and shares the wisdom, stories, energy, and inspiration of something that is truly extraordinary.

—TAI J. MENDENHALL, PH.D., LMFT, CFT
ASSISTANT PROFESSOR
DEPARTMENT OF FAMILY SOCIAL SCIENCE
UNIVERSITY OF MINNESOTA, TWIN CITIES

I highly recommend this book as a text for post-secondary international development and social work courses. Students will learn strategies for starting, growing, and running an international developmen t organization; working with local communities on projects to improve their quality of life; harnessing people and resources to achieve goals across national and cultural boundaries; and achieving significant health and well-being outcomes for some of the world's poorest families.

—CATHERINE A. SOLHEIM
ASSOCIATE PROFESSOR
DEPARTMENT OF FAMILY SOCIAL SCIENCE
UNIVERSITY OF MINNESOTA

Insistence on community investment and direction is critical to the success of Mano a Mano. *Gaining Ground* documents this history and process, providing a structure and process for others to implement. This book is a valuable resource for courses in social work, community development, international social services, nonprofit administration, and international development, especially those that are focused on nongovernmental organizations.

—CAROL F. KUECHLER, PH.D.
PROGRAM DIRECTOR
MSW SCHOOL OF SOCIAL WORK
ST. CATHERINE UNIVERSITY/ UNIVERSITY OF ST. THOMAS

# TABLE OF CONTENTS

# Introduction

The phrase *losing ground* is often used to describe failed efforts to reduce poverty and disease in developing countries. *Gaining Ground* tells a different story.

This is the story of how a small, volunteer-based organization—Mano a Mano International Partners—has steadily and dramatically improved health and economic well-being in one of the poorest corners of the world. Launched at a kitchen table in Mendota Heights, Minnesota, and sustained by persons with stout hearts and strong backs, Mano a Mano has in just twenty years dramatically transformed the lives of hundreds of thousands of the world's poorest citizens: the residents of Bolivia's most remote villages.

Those astonished by and curious about how a small medical recycling project could gain so much ground so quickly have sought Mano a Mano's guidance and assistance to replicate its success elsewhere. This book responds to those requests.

Twenty years after its modest starting point, Mano a Mano finds itself uniquely situated to offer counsel and encouragement. Its experiences in Bolivia have differed markedly from those of many other nonprofits with similar humanitarian objectives.

This book shares success stories and best practices. The story of this small Minnesota nonprofit is about going beyond preconceived notions of how things are supposed to be done. Mano a Mano's successful model of participatory development is not a product of conventional international development literature or research into U.S.-based nonprofit practices. Rather this model has evolved as a result of ongoing experience, careful stewardship, and common sense. The Mano a Mano community-based model, which rejects conventional top-down approaches in favor of trust and reliance on grassroots expertise, has achieved a level of success that is most dramatically illustrated by concrete data.

In 1994 Mano a Mano volunteers collected and distributed 500 pounds of medical surplus to Bolivia and thought they had really achieved something. No one dreamed then that in the following twenty years the organization would do so much more. Mano a Mano has built clinics, schools, roads, reservoirs, and airstrips—and all are still intact, well maintained, and operational. Today Mano a Mano staff and volunteers are not only continuing to collect and distribute medical surplus (over three million pounds to date), but also engaging in:

- Building, equipping, and staffing clinics (145 of them so far, almost all of which are now self-sustaining).

- Building schools, teacher-housing, and sanitation facilities (now in over forty-nine villages).

- Creating and operating an aviation program that has airlifted more than 2,166 critically ill or injured persons to city hospitals and transported Mano a Mano staff and volunteers to serve in otherwise inaccessible regions.

- Building airstrips (twenty-one so far).

- Improving or constructing over 1,400 kilometers of roads through otherwise impassable terrain.

- Building water projects that have helped rural communities manage their limited water supplies, strategies that have transformed regional economies. To date, Mano a Mano has built seven major agricultural water reservoirs and 170 smaller holding ponds, which together have increased crop production and improved food security for over 30,000 people.

As a result of Mano a Mano's efforts, more than 700,000 Bolivians have access to health care for the first time. Infant and maternal mortality rates in Mano a Mano clinics are dramatically lower than the averages for rural Bolivia. Roads reduce travel time from days to mere hours for people in isolated communities to reach medical care.

From the beginning, Mano a Mano has been virtually an all-volunteer organization. Hundreds of U.S. and Bolivian volunteers are the troops on the ground. Volunteers collect, sort, transport, store, and distribute inventory. Volunteers finish, furnish, and open new clinics. Volunteers sell Bolivian crafts, organize fundraising campaigns, cook at picnics, write newsletters, and speak to church and civic groups. Volunteers helped design and continue to help manage a website. One Bolivian volunteer who said, "Mano a Mano is my religion," articulated the shared commitment of many Mano a Mano volunteers to the organization's mission. In short, volunteerism has been the lifeblood of Mano a Mano. It was four years before the organization was able to pay a dedicated Bolivian manager who had already been volunteering every weekend. Ten years passed before the organization had the means to hire U.S. staff members to spearhead what had long been overwhelming volunteer responsibilities.

Thus, this is the story of a volunteer army. But every army needs its generals and Mano a Mano has had the best. No international effort can succeed without dedicated leaders in its target country—people who are unfailingly honest, talented, and tireless. In Bolivia those leaders have emerged from the Velásquez family. Beginning with José Velásquez and soon extending to his wife Cinthia, his brother Ivo, his sister María Blanca, and then each successive generation, this book describes the indispensable role the Velásquez family has played in all Mano a Mano initiatives in Bolivia.

However, none have been more central to Mano a Mano's development and success than its founders, Segundo Velásquez and Joan Swanson Velásquez. Mano a Mano volunteers describe Joan and Segundo as the organization's "heart and soul."

Segundo, the third oldest of his siblings, was born in Laguna Carmen, a village so poor and isolated that its residents speak Quechua, the indigenous language of Bolivia, rather than Spanish. To understand the Velásquez children's later achievements, it is necessary to appreciate the extraordinary courage it took for their parents to recognize that Laguna Carmen, the only place they knew, offered no future and that they must move to the city. Segundo remembers the early years in Cochabamba, currently the fourth largest city in Bolivia, as a time of desperate poverty. They all tirelessly scrounged to support the family. Little by little, the Velásquez family gained an economic toehold. First they made cement tiles. Then, after the purchase of a barely functioning truck, they were able to buy and transport water to the hillside, where they sold it at a small profit to even poorer barrio residents. Other tools and skills followed, and Segundo grew up convinced that if he just had a hammer and pliers, he could do anything.

Then came Joan. The couple met when Joan was a Peace Corps volunteer in Bolivia. Segundo moved to the United States, where he trained as an aviation technician. He eventually finished college, became a technical manager at Northwest

Airlines, married Joan, and enjoyed the good life. However, Segundo remained stunned by the riches—and waste—he saw in the United States, and he never forgot where he came from. He felt destined to give back.

At age two Joan had contracted polio, which led to full-body paralysis and several weeks in an iron lung. Through the generosity of her neighbors in the tiny farming community of Valley Springs, South Dakota, she spent the year that included her third birthday at the Mayo Clinic in Rochester, Minnesota. Joan's social conscience was stoked in the early years not only by her ongoing health struggles, but also by a landowner's callous treatment of her tenant farmer parents. Joan has experienced poverty, physical challenges, and unfairness; and she has spent her life tackling each.

After graduating from Western Reserve University in Cleveland, Ohio in 1965 with a degree in social work, Joan visited three doctors before one would sign off on her joining the Peace Corps. Despite her respiratory problems, Joan was assigned to the high altitudes of Bolivia. In fact, nothing about the posting was easy. Joan found her assigned project cancelled due to revolution in the region. Undaunted, she stayed and established a day-care center in a poor barrio on the outskirts of Cochabamba. (It operates to this day.)

After returning to the U.S., Joan earned her doctorate in social work and pursued a successful career in administration and research. However, in 1994 her health challenges proved to be too much to manage. Suffering from post-polio syndrome, Joan was forced to take a medical leave. Flat on her back and on oxygen most of the time, Joan used her many months of bed rest to lay the groundwork for Mano a Mano. Operating under the theory that although her body wasn't cooperating, there was nothing wrong with her mind, she decided to use this time to help Segundo fulfill his passion to give back to Bolivia. Mano a Mano likely would not exist if Joan's health had allowed her to continue her professional career. Ironically, since those early months of forced bed rest, Joan and Segundo have each devoted forty or more hours per week over nearly twenty years, always unpaid, to Mano a Mano and its mission. At 4'11" tall, Joan stands as a giant.

Joan and Segundo have been recognized for what they initiated and all the achievements they have overseen. Segundo's presence on stage with former vice president Al Gore at the 2009 United Nations Millennium Development Goals conference brought international attention to the organization. Since then it has become evident that Mano a Mano is one of very few organizations that has made real progress toward achieving the Millennium Goals. In 2012, Segundo was one of three finalists for the Opus Prize, an honor that resulted in a substantial contribution to Mano a Mano. In 2008, Joan was awarded the National Peace Corps Association's prestigious Sargent Shriver Award for Distinguished Humanitarian Service. Upon accepting the award, she explained why she and Segundo have devoted their lives to helping others rise from poverty:

> The spirit of international volunteerism moved Segundo and me to create Mano a Mano, founding it on the premise that a group of determined volunteers could reach across national boundaries to make a real difference in the lives of others. From its very humble beginnings—collecting a few surgical instruments for a hospital in Cochabamba, Bolivia—Mano a Mano has grown far beyond our capacity to imagine. Seven hundred thousand rural Bolivians who subsist on less than one dollar per day now have access to health care for the first time in their lives because Mano a Mano has clinics in their villages. Thousands have a reliable water supply for their crops and livestock, and a road on which to transport them to market because Mano a Mano has built roads and reservoirs with them... We hope that our story inspires others to join us on this journey; just as we have been inspired by those who believed that a few committed people can change the world.

Joan wrote this book to respond to the many requests Mano a Mano has received from international humanitarian nonprofits and nongovernmental organizations (NGOs) for guidance. While Bolivia's ongoing needs and daunting challenges prevent Mano a Mano from expanding into new ventures—however exciting and compelling they might be—this book offers an account of one organization's humble beginnings and its growth into an organization that makes an ongoing and dramatic difference in a developing country. The hope is that others will take the best of the Mano a Mano experience, shape it to meet their particular needs and circumstances, and then tackle the challenges of acute poverty in other corners of the world.

Christine Ver Ploeg
St. Paul, Minnesota, April 2014

# 1

# Good Intentions

*A good intention clothes itself with sudden power.*
—Ralph Waldo Emerson[1]

For us, the call to action was personal. Born to Bolivian peasant parents, Segundo knew firsthand the hardships faced by families in the rural villages high in the Andes. For me, insights came secondhand through a Peace Corps assignment.

A land of scenic grandeur that includes the Andes Mountains and the Amazon River basin, Bolivia lends itself to superlatives: the world's largest protected wetland system (Llanos de Moxos),[2] the world's most extensive tropical rain forest (Amazon basin),[3] the world's largest salt flats (Salar de Uyuni),[4] the world's highest commercially navigable lake (Lake Titicaca),[5] and the world's highest capital city (La Paz).[6] Bolivia's mountains, its rain forests, and its wetlands are home to more than 1,400 species of birds.[7] Bolivia is rich in petroleum and natural gas. Its mineral resources include iron ore, silver, zinc, and tin. One of the world's largest lithium deposits lies underneath the Uyuni salt flats.[8]

Alongside its natural beauty, Bolivia has preserved its history and heritage. Bolivia's largest population segment is composed of Amerindians.[9] In Bolivia there are thirty-six indigenous groups whose links to particular regions go back thousands of years and whose languages are recognized as official.[10] But Bolivia's majestic vistas, its diversity of plant and animal life, its wealth of mineral and energy resources, and its rich cultural history do not tell the whole story. Landlocked since 1904,[11] Bolivia is South America's poorest nation.[12] With a total population just over ten million, more than half the people of Bolivia live in deep material poverty.[13] Family incomes average less than a dollar a day.[14] The country's wealth is concentrated in its cities. But even the cities are poor; almost half of Bolivia's city dwellers (43.5 percent) live in poor barrios.[15] Outside the cities it's worse. The same vistas that garner rave reviews dictate isolation and economic hardship for many rural Bolivians. Approximately a third of Bolivia's population (an estimated 3.3 million people) reside in rural areas.[16] Of this rural population, more than sixty-five percent do not have sufficient income to cover basic needs.[17]

Bolivia was not always landlocked. Until the War of the Pacific (1879–84) with Chile and the treaty that followed (1904), Bolivia owned 250 miles of coastline. In April 2013 Bolivia filed suit in the International Court of Justice in The Hague in an attempt to regain this coastline.[18] While access to coastal ports might provide advantages relating to foreign investment and commerce with a corresponding effect on GDP and average per capita income, it is difficult to imagine much direct effect on rural Bolivians. Their improved lives and livelihoods depend on other factors. Some rural residents work as miners or artisans, but the vast majority eke out a meager living as subsistence farmers, raising crops and a few domestic animals on one- or two-acre plots. The climate and terrain present challenges. As a consequence, 37 percent of rural children under age five suffer from chronic malnutrition.[19]

## Rural Poverty in Bolivia and Its Effects

Villagers in Bolivia's rural countryside want something else for their children despite familial loyalties and ancient traditions. In this respect, many villagers are like Segundo's family.

When a new school was built in Jatun K'asa, villagers from neighboring villages willingly sent their children. Instead of making the three-hour walk each morning to school and the return three-hour trek home each evening, twenty children stayed overnight and were housed in the old school building. The families sent a week's supply of potatoes with these children, some as young as six years old, who were then responsible for gathering firewood, cooking the evening meal, sleeping in crude living quarters, and managing on their own. The story of these schoolchildren demonstrates the accustomed standard of living and the commitment of rural villagers to find a better path for future generations.

Life expectancy in Bolivia has increased in the last sixty years. Figures for 1960–2012 show an increase in the average life expectancy from forty-two to sixty-seven years of age.[20] However, this gain was seen primarily in urban areas. Poverty is greater in the rural areas, and poverty affects longevity. For rural villagers the lack of healthy food, clean drinking water, and available health care contribute significantly to shortened life spans.

The impact of Bolivia's pervasive rural poverty falls especially hard on mothers and their children. Though maternal death rates have decreased during the last two decades from 416 to 310 per 100,000, this improvement has occurred primarily in urban areas.[21] While acknowledging that health data for rural Bolivia is incomplete, comparing estimated rural maternal, infant, and child mortality rates with urban statistics illustrates startling disparities. An estimated 524 rural women die for every 100,000 births, while the death rate for urban women is approximately half that number—274 deaths for 100,000 births.[22] While 7.5 percent of rural infants in Bolivia die within one month of birth, the rate for urban infants is 4.3 percent.[23] Ten percent of rural children die before age five, compared to five percent of their urban counterparts.[24] Comparisons to what Americans perceive as normal maternal and infant mortality provide perspective. In the United States, 12.7 mothers die for every 100,000 births and the infant mortality rate is 0.7 percent.[25]

Bolivia's literacy rate (86.7 percent) is among the lowest for Latin American countries.[26] The average length of schooling for Bolivians is 5.6 years,[27] and there is a huge disparity for students from urban and rural areas; people aged twenty-five to sixty-five from urban areas average 9.98 years of school versus only 4.85 years of school for people aged twenty-five to sixty-five from rural areas.[28] Nearly 50 percent of students drop out before finishing primary school to work in the fields or in the mines, or to care for younger children.[29] While Bolivian law requires that children ages seven through fourteen attend school,[30] many parents and children simply cannot comply.

Many rural schools consist of dilapidated buildings, one-room adobe structures without doors or windows. Some schools are simply benches under trees. Most rural schools lack the most basic supplies and furnishings, and rarely have access to electricity. Such environments create nearly insurmountable obstacles to teaching and learning. Rural villages find it difficult to recruit teachers and almost impossible to retain them for more than a few weeks. Parents report that teachers sent to their rural communities often abandon their posts and go to the city for weeks at a time because they cannot endure the harsh conditions. A teacher at the school in Jatun K'asa reported finding rats and snakes in the school building in another village. He said he awoke one morning to find a tarantula on his chest.

Parents in rural Bolivia believe education provides an escape from poverty and they desperately seek solutions to the current challenges of education in their communities.

## History of Good Intentions

Charitable impulses have a long history. The tithe and the zakat exist as a matter of law and time-honored tradition. Through tithes, public aid, and charitable donations a country's wealth has historically been shared with those less fortunate. As early as the nineteenth century, people of good will formed organizations to serve the public good.[31]

Prior to 1970, charitable work in Bolivia involved mainly emergency relief and mission work. Few nongovernmental organizations (NGOs) operated in Bolivia until thirty years ago.[32] Since the 1980s, however, the number has increased dramatically. Today more than 600 NGOs operate in Bolivia to serve charitable ends.[33]

## Desperate Need: Lingering Poverty in Rural Bolivia

Bolivia's mortality and literacy numbers have improved. But most analysts who review the statistics conclude that virtually all the improvement in those figures reflects gains made in urban areas.[34] Historically, almost all the NGOs active in Bolivia have operated to benefit the urban and peri-urban populations.[35] Those NGOs' worthy efforts deserve acclaim, but the plight of rural villagers demands urgent attention.

Geographic and economic circumstances make it nearly impossible for most rural Bolivian families to protect their health, educate their children, and improve their standard of living. If a documented need exists in the rural areas, it is reasonable to ask why more hasn't been done. Of the many contributing factors, geography ranks near the top of the list.

In May 1998 a series of earthquakes near Aiquile (population 5,000), a town in the Carrasco province, resulted in an estimated sixty deaths from landslides.[36] In the aftermath of the quake, the Bolivian government used flyovers to assess the damage and discover where help was needed. One unintended result of the rescue efforts was the Bolivian government's discovery of many villages that had previously been undocumented and uncharted.

Segundo grew up in rural Bolivia. His birthplace, the village of Laguna Carmen (population 100), is located in a mountain valley. Laguna Carmen resembles most other Bolivian villages; the same families have lived there for generations. Like most other villagers, Segundo's parents were subsistence farmers.

The phrase *off the map* is an idiomatic expression used figuratively to designate a place far removed from civilization or currently out of existence. The phrase applies literally to Bolivian villages: Laguna Carmen is literally off the map. If you try to run an internet search for it, you will fail. If you search through Bolivian guidebooks, you will come up short. If you peruse printed maps of Bolivia, you will find no such place.

The nearest towns to Laguna Carmen are Punata and Cliza. Although Laguna Carmen is only five kilometers (3.1 miles) from Punata, the route is challenging. The village is essentially cut off from both towns and from the arterial road system that links the two. Thousands of other rural Bolivian villages share similar circumstances. Villagers are isolated. Subsistence farming is hard work, and the villagers' days are long. Interaction with villagers from neighboring communities is infrequent.

The same geography that impedes interaction between rural communities makes charitable intervention challenging. Bolivia's difficult geography makes it hard for an NGO to even identify a community where a clinic or school might have a chance of success. The same geographical challenges complicate construction efforts, staffing, supply, and long-term sustainability.

Travel between villages is time-consuming and often treacherous. Some villages are precariously situated on mountainsides. Others, like Laguna Carmen, are located in valleys surrounded by mountains. Getting to an arterial road might require hours of hiking along rocky paths through the mountains. Some Bolivian villages can only be reached by boat.

Bolivia has about 80,488 kilometers (48,300 miles) of road.[37] Only 6,841 kilometers (4,104 miles)—less than 8.5 percent—are paved. [38] Although La Paz, Santa Cruz, and Cochabamba are connected by paved highways, some experienced drivers have described them as "horrible." Most roads have plenty of potholes but little signage. Bridges may be washed out, and drivers may encounter waterfalls, mudslides, landslides, and avalanches—not to mention inexperienced drivers. Roads through the mountains are often only wide enough for one vehicle. Even where there are extreme drop-offs, Bolivian highways do not usually offer shoulders or guardrails. An ascending vehicle has the right of way. That means any descending vehicle must back up the road until it finds a shelf that allows the other vehicle to pass. Also, even the best mountain roads have dangerous blind turns.

## Barriers to Rural Development

In addition to the inherent geographical difficulties that challenge rural Bolivia, other factors also stand in the way of rural development.

Historically, the Amerindian communities of Bolivia dealt with outsiders through brokers or spokesmen.[39] Even today, if an NGO or individual approaches a rural community with plans for good deeds, a threshold issue is overcoming the suspicion afforded a stranger, who is likely to evoke a measure of distrust.

Language is another barrier. To operate in Bolivia, NGOs usually employ bilingual staff members with fluency in Spanish. That works in the context of urban and possibly peri-urban development projects. Out in the rural communities, it may be necessary to work with an interpreter who speaks Quechua, Aymara, or another Amerindian language.

Bolivian national politics and diplomatic relations also complicate the work of NGOs, particularly those with a U.S. connection. In 2008, U.S. President George W. Bush signaled his intention to suspend trade preferences to pressure Bolivia to do more to stop the flow of drugs from the country.[40] Conflicting political agendas between the United States and Bolivia relate not only to the drug trade, but also to a range of other issues, which can have a direct impact on NGOs.

In September 2008, Bolivia ordered the U.S. ambassador, Philip S. Goldberg, to leave the country after accusing him of supporting rebellious factions.[41] Two months later, the government expelled U.S. Drug Enforcement Agency (DEA) agents.[42] Despite the normalization of diplomatic relations announced in November 2011, the DEA was not invited to return.[43] More recently, on May 1, 2013, Bolivia expelled the U.S. Agency for International Development (USAID), saying the organization had conspired against the government.[44]

These events are just a sampling of the difficulties in diplomatic relations between the United States and Bolivia in recent years, and NGOs get swept up in the process; many NGOs that relied heavily on USAID funding were forced to reduce their programs or shut down completely. For Mano a Mano, the USAID shipping programs that provided hundreds of thousands of dollars' worth of shipments were no longer available; since 2011, this has meant an additional fundraising burden of $100,000 to 200,000 *each year* to continue the surplus distribution program. Occasionally, the negative press about Bolivia in the United States (which rarely goes beyond the headlines showing challenges in relations between the two governments) can impact potential supporters' interest, and the negative associations of the United States in Bolivia can impact relationships with community leaders or government officials. These challenges offer yet another example of the importance of building capacity in-country; Mano a Mano is not a U.S.-based NGO with an office in Bolivia, but rather a Bolivian NGO (with Bolivian staff and board, and Bolivian registration) that receives support from an NGO in the United States. This fundamental difference has helped Mano a Mano continue to operate and avoid many (though not all) of the momentous challenges that other NGOs have had to face.

Like other developing countries, Bolivia has had a serious problem with bribes and other corrupt practices in the past.[45] Since taking office in 2006, President Evo Morales has declared a zero-tolerance policy against corruption,[46] and in 2010 an anti-corruption law was enacted.[47] It is too soon to judge what effect these efforts may have on NGO activities in Bolivia.

## Finding the Means To Do Good

Some may be disheartened by the political climate in Bolivia, by the possibility of confronting corruption, and by bad roads that stop short of the destination. Good works are not always easy—but the needs in rural Bolivia are compelling. This book documents Mano a Mano's search for a means to address those needs; it describes the earnest intentions that started it all and documents the will and resolution that translated those intentions into good deeds.

# 2

# Creation of Mano a Mano

*Success is not final, failure is not fatal. It is the courage to continue that counts.*
**—Attributed to Winston Churchill**

Initially, Segundo and I had no intention of forming a non-profit. We simply wanted to transport handheld medical instruments and easy-to-move supplies, such as gauze and gloves, to medical professionals in Bolivia who lacked the most basic items. We assumed some organization out there must have been doing just that already, and we expected to work through them.

A friend provided a list of over ninety organizations that address international health issues. Surely one of them would welcome our donations and earmark them for Bolivia. Or so we thought. Unfortunately, our initial confidence faded as one phone call after another ended with the words, "We can't help you, but we wish you the best." Not easily dissuaded, Segundo and I concluded that if we wanted to collect medical surplus for use in Bolivia, we would have to oversee the challenge from beginning to end.

For many years, Segundo had been carrying small medical donations to Bolivia when he visited his family. Through his extensive personal contacts with Bolivian health-care providers, he could see firsthand the desperate need and how quickly the gifts were put to use. Segundo also came to see with increasing clarity that many Minnesota hospitals and clinics store and then discard usable supplies, instruments, and equipment simply because they cannot afford to pay staff to sort the items and prepare them for use or resale.

Having failed to find a nonprofit entity willing to serve as a channel for medical donations, Segundo and I were left with only two choices. We could continue to informally accept small donations and carry them to Bolivia in our luggage. Or we could create a nonprofit organization, seek larger donations, and try to raise funds to ship them to the areas of greatest need. A chance encounter at a wedding reception helped decide the question.

While chatting at the reception with a respiratory therapist who worked for a large hospital and outpatient network, we mentioned our interest in collecting medical surplus. With her insider's knowledge, the therapist suggested that we could obtain large donations if we formed a nonprofit. Even at that early stage we understood that we'd need to demonstrate both the capacity and accountability to handle donations responsibly and ensure the donated goods weren't misused or sold. Our new friend offered to help us find donation sources if we incorporated a nonprofit and obtained tax-exempt status.

This serendipitous meeting proved to be the tipping point. Our determination to transform medical waste into desperately needed inventory that could potentially save lives inspired others to join our effort. Within four months, we had a name for our organization and an idea for how it would work. We called the organization Mano a Mano (*hand to hand* in Spanish) Medical Resources—now often shortened to simply Mano a Mano or Mano a Mano U.S. In the first four months, we formed a nine-member board of directors, filed all the necessary not-for-profit paperwork, created a program structure, and produced a cut-and-paste pamphlet. Without the help and wise counsel of family and friends, none of it could have happened.

## Foundational Principles

Some might characterize our preparations as naïve. Segundo and I didn't begin by delving into the ample body of literature on international development, by researching best practices, or by drawing on the experiences of U.S.-based nonprofits that work in the international arena. Instead, we drew on our own lives and professional experience.

As an airline industry veteran with twenty years of experience in corporate governance, Segundo was adept at managing fast-paced technical work in which both precision and timeliness are critical to success. The fact that Segundo is trilingual (English, Spanish, and Quechua) and tricultural was essential as we considered how to move forward.

Before my retirement in 1994, I used my doctorate in social work for thirty years in the field. My professional experience, which was varied, included governance, program development, and research. Having lived in Bolivia as a Peace Corps volunteer in the 1960s, I am also bilingual (English and Spanish). Social-work theory, values, principles, and practices profoundly influenced my Peace Corps work and laid the foundation for the formation of Mano a Mano. As I considered how my Peace Corps experience might inform our proposed charitable undertaking in Bolivia, I relied on what I viewed as the first principle underpinning my Peace Corps project: *get to know the other.*

In 1967, I joined the Peace Corps and was sent to work in Bolivia. The assignment I chose involved work with a Catholic parish, defining and putting into practice a yet-to-be-selected project in a desperately poor barrio of about one hundred families on the outskirts of Cochabamba.

Saul Alinsky, a community organizer who emphasized the importance of involving those one hopes to help, once wrote,

"Start by getting to know the other's point of view."[48] Recalling Alinsky's writings, I spent the first two weeks in Cochabamba visiting every one- and two-room adobe home in the barrio. My efforts to connect to the parish gave me the advantage of being accepted as part of the community rather than viewed as a stranger.

People were happy to share their stories. The barrio's parents worried most about the care of their young children. While a mother could carry a baby on her back and possibly manage a toddler when she left home in the early morning to sell in the open market, her other children were left home alone. The children were locked into their homes so no harm would come to them. Tragedy struck when a five-year-old decided to prepare dinner and her dress caught on fire. Frantic neighbors heard her screams, but she died before they could save her. Every family shared this story with me. None of them had heard of day-care centers. But when I described the concept to them, they embraced it. Within two months the center was open and caring for fifty preschool children.

All Mano a Mano projects are based on that same foundational principle: get to know the other. Through firsthand experience, I am convinced that this tenet is fundamental to successful cross-cultural humanitarian efforts.

## Social Work and Human Rights Principles

The social work profession's values and principles[49] permeate and shape every aspect of Mano a Mano's mission, development, and growth. From the beginning, Mano a Mano has intentionally developed programs from the ground up rather than the top down, engaging the communities it serves as full partners. Mano a Mano consistently attends to cultural differences, working to achieve a harmonious balance between the U.S. tendency to focus on efficiency and task completion and Latino culture, which attends to relationships first.

Social work's respect for the worth and dignity of all human beings compels social workers to defend all persons' rights to have their basic physical and emotional needs met. International human rights declarations and conventions form common standards of achievement and recognize rights that are accepted by the global community, including Mano a Mano. In its formal "Statement of Principles," the International Federation of Social Workers identifies key human rights precepts that remain at the core of our organization's mission.[50]

## RESPECTING THE RIGHT TO SELF-DETERMINATION—TO MAKE ONE'S OWN CHOICES AS LONG AS THEY DON'T INJURE OTHERS.

When Mano a Mano initiated its medical surplus program, we focused on gathering donations to fill the supply and equipment needs expressed by hospital and outpatient clinic staff in Cochabamba. Each subsequent program has been developed in response to a direct need and request from a community.

## PROMOTING THE RIGHT TO PARTICIPATION—INVOLVING PEOPLE IN WAYS THAT REINFORCE THEIR CAPACITIES TO MAKE DECISIONS AND TAKE ACTIONS TO IMPROVE THEIR LIVES.

Mano a Mano includes community members in all aspects of planning, building, and managing its projects. They participate as equal and essential partners and develop an intense sense of ownership of their projects. Their engagement and ownership has proven critical to long-term sustainability.

## TREATING EACH PERSON AS A WHOLE WITHIN AN INTERRELATED FAMILY, COMMUNITY, SOCIETAL, AND NATURAL ENVIRONMENT.

Mano a Mano recognizes the complex, interrelated factors that contribute to improved health and economic development. Teaching public health and good hygiene practices in addition to treating illness, for example, accounts for the web of factors that influence improved health.

**IDENTIFYING AND DEVELOPING STRENGTHS—RECOGNIZING THAT ALL INDIVIDUALS AND FAMILIES HAVE STRENGTHS AND RESOURCES WHICH THEY CAN LEARN TO TAP AS THEY ADDRESS ISSUES AND CHALLENGES.**

The families with whom Mano a Mano works live in extreme material poverty, but show strong motivation to change their life circumstances. Community residents contribute all the unskilled labor required to complete a project in partnership with Mano a Mano. They learn to mix cement, help lay bricks, and organize themselves into work crews. The organization builds on their resourcefulness and creativity to teach new skills that they can apply to other projects and issues throughout their lives.

## Cross-Cultural Partnerships

As Mano a Mano's founders, Segundo and I worked to create an organization that would develop partnership connections between Minnesota and Bolivia. From the outset we recognized both the richness and the challenges involved in cross-cultural encounters.[51] At first a bicultural framework informed every choice, and the bicultural essence of the organization continues to infuse decisions, directions, and achievements.

Culture, by definition, is a set of values, norms, and beliefs shared by an identifiable group of people at a point in time. Three cultural groups came to play an integral role with Mano a Mano: the dominant culture of Minnesota that is heavily influenced by its Scandinavian and German roots, the dominant Hispanic culture of urban Bolivia, and the dominant rural Bolivian culture of the Quechuas. Each culture has recognizable boundaries for standards of conduct, some of which reflect conflicting underlying values. When members of one group act in a manner that is expected and accepted in their culture, they can easily violate the standards of the other without recognizing what has occurred.

Here's an example: a twenty-five year-old Bolivian man completed a course in auto mechanics and received an offer of employment in a faraway city. Because the offer included an excellent salary and housing, his visiting instructor from the United States assumed the student would be elated and accept the offer. Instead the student told the instructor that he'd have to consult his mother. When the student turned down the offer because of the distance from home, the instructor became angry, called the student a "baby tied to his mother's apron strings" and retracted further help in the quest for employment. The student did not understand his instructor's reaction. In his relationship-based culture, his mother would continue to be the most significant person throughout his life. He could not ignore his responsibility toward her.

Effective cross-cultural work requires that at least one person involved in each component relationship be able to function within both cultural contexts. The instructor in this example had traveled to another country to teach its students. It was his responsibility to learn to effectively interact within the culture he had entered.

An individual who recognizes the nuanced values, standards of conduct, and beliefs of a culture that differs from his or her own and can function fully within that culture is considered bicultural. Reaching the point of full functionality in two cultures requires much more than speaking the language. It depends on enthusiastically taking every opportunity to observe, interact, and consciously analyze. A truly multicultural individual moves back and forth among cultures with ease, while fully recognizing and appreciating the differences and accepting every culture as legitimate.

Mano a Mano's board members and volunteers have worked assiduously to observe, analyze, and respect the cultural differences that permeate and inform the organization's objectives and everyday interactions. Together we have worked hard to assure that the organization itself is truly multicultural.

## Creating the 501(c)(3) Organization

In October 1994, a small group of dedicated volunteers gathered around our kitchen table in Mendota Heights, Minnesota. Working together, we created Mano a Mano, a 501(c)(3) organization founded on the simple proposition that medical inventory that would otherwise be wasted in the United States should be routed to places where it could mean the difference between life and death. As a group, we undertook certain practical steps to initiate the organization's beginning stages, which we now refer to as Phase I (1994–96).

Working together, we drafted incorporation, policy, and tax-exempt documents. We selected qualified individuals to serve on the board of directors. We developed a reliable accounting system. We filed the Mano a Mano articles of incorporation and bylaws with the state of Minnesota. We applied to the Internal Revenue Service (IRS) for tax-exempt status. Each of these organizational steps was vital. Passionate about our cause, we went to great lengths to get it right. Certain steps, we realized, assume extra importance in the context of an international, cross-cultural mission.

A more detailed look at Mano a Mano's initial formation follows.

**1. Draft incorporation, policy, and tax-exempt documents.**

I began by reading do-it-yourself books for start-up foundations, federal registers, and informational materials I requested from government offices. In truth, I read anything that might point a new organization in the right direction. I carefully studied state regulations available through the Minnesota secretary of state's and attorney general's offices. Each state makes its own rules for forming and regulating nonprofits and has a wealth of information available on articles of incorporation, bylaws, financial reporting, fundraising, and exemption from sales and real estate taxes.

State officials and colleagues who worked for other charitable organizations provided helpful examples of articles of incorporation and bylaws. Incorporation is usually the first step for a not-for-profit entity. "Articles of incorporation" is the name for the basic charter used to establish the existence of the organization. This document sets out the name of the organization, its purpose, and other information mandated by state statute. Bylaws provide the day-to-day rules of operation. The requirement to file bylaws varies from state to state. If not required to do so, an organization may elect to file its bylaws with the designated state office and make them public documents to demonstrate its accountability and transparency. It is required that the bylaws be kept on hand by the organization and made available on request to government agencies.

Taking inspiration from among the most relevant examples, I drafted both documents for Mano a Mano. Future board members helped me identify essential information, which I then codified in general terms while avoiding too much detail that might later prove confining. This approach served Mano a Mano well given the relatively rapid expansion of its programs.

With continued input from interested supporters, I also prepared a set of board policies, internal documents that guide the conduct of the board and its oversight of the organization. These policies fell into three categories: governance, executive limitation, and finances. They include, for example, the conflict-of-interest policy that is recommended by the Minnesota

Charities Review Council. Mano a Mano's board of directors revisits and updates these policies periodically on a simple majority vote.

The IRS was the key source of information for preparing to file for tax-exempt status. I read every word and struggled to decipher federal publications that describe Internal Revenue Code (IRC) section 501(c)(3), the official designation obtained for tax-exempt status. These materials provided essential guidance on receipt, valuation, and accounting for in-kind gifts and on charitable gift deductions.

Public libraries and government offices have up-to-date editions of useful sources. Most offer those materials online for easy access.

It is important to gain a thorough understanding of legal requirements and regulations before attempting to incorporate an organization. Mano a Mano avoided many potential problems by laying the groundwork carefully. A significant example relates to the IRS requirement that a nonprofit organization receiving in-kind gifts place a defensible value on each gift. The nonprofit must report the true value of in-kind gifts on its annual report to the IRS; it's not sufficient to simply assign the donor's assertion of the gift's value.

During the early years, in-kind donations of medical items comprised the major portion of gifts to Mano a Mano. The IRS requirement raised questions that seemed to have no answer. What is the value of a half-full box of individually wrapped syringes? Or a box of gloves after a fall from the loading dock, if that fall damaged its outer packaging? Or unused items from a surgical kit?

We resolved these questions before accepting donations. We went directly to a key source, a member of the IRS nonprofit division who gave us invaluable guidance. She advised us to get the best cost estimates possible from manufacturers, discount them for broken or incomplete boxes or any other damage or issue created by incomplete kits, and write down the rationale for any discounted valuation. Following this advice, volunteers obtained cost figures for a wide variety of new supplies from a hospital and worked with me to establish a discounted rate for each article. We contacted a distributor of used medical equipment for prices on durable items. Using the discounted rate for supplies (all of which were new) and the used rate for equipment, we created a value structure that remains in use and continues to be expanded and updated. Auditors and the IRS examiners have accepted that schedule each year without question. Failure to create a defensible system could have impeded our ability to obtain and maintain Mano a Mano's tax-exempt status.

## MANO A MANO'S FOUNDING MISSION:

To increase the capacity of health-care providers in Bolivia to serve impoverished patients.

## OUR PHILOSOPHY:

| | |
|---|---|
| Volunteerism | Empowerment |
| Frugality | Flexibility |
| Competence | Respect |
| Partnership with communities | Accountability |

## 2. Select a board of directors.

As founders, we approached the task of selecting a board by searching the public library for books on nonprofit boards and drawing lessons from those accounts, talking with board members of other organizations, and then meeting with friends who were executive directors of nonprofits. After synthesizing their advice, we decided to seek board members with the following qualifications:

- Knowledge and skills that would be useful in the creation of a well-functioning, credible organization. In addition to the founders, both of whom had governance and program development experience in large organizations, the original board included an attorney, a certified public accountant, and a physician who had years of experience working with a Latino population.

- Reputation for integrity (e.g., evidence that an individual had earned a high level of respect as a public official)

- Bilingual (Spanish/English) language skills and bicultural experience

- A demonstrated passion for creating a more just world

- Capacity to work well in a relatively informal team environment

- Willingness to volunteer expertise to the organization

We wrote a board member job description and began contacting people we knew either to serve on the board or to recommend others. Through this process we identified nine individuals who, working together, addressed the task of creating and incorporating Mano a Mano.

**3. Create an accounting system.**

It fell to me to create the original accounting system. I turned to accounting texts for nonprofits and the assistance of the accountant on the board to help create a chart of accounts and a manual accounting system. After working for a year with the manual system, Mano a Mano felt ready to computerize it and purchased a QuickBooks software package. As the types of projects expanded and the number of counterparts increased, the system became much more complex, but the original framework continued to serve us well.

**4. File articles of incorporation and bylaws with the state and apply to the IRS for tax-exempt status.**

The secretary of state's office provides the proper forms and can explain what other paperwork must be filed. That office also advised us on the required fees. The IRS provides tax benefits to organizations that qualify for status as charitable organizations under IRC 501(c)(3). Organizations begin the determination process by filing Form 1023 with the IRS. As a prerequisite to filing Form 1023, the organization must be organized as a trust, an association, or a corporation and must have an Employer Identification Number (EIN), for which there is a filing fee. Upon a determination that the applicant meets the organization requirements under IRC 501(c)(3), the IRS sends an approval letter that sets out the favorable determination of the organization's qualified status. The organization retains this letter in its permanent records as proof of its tax-exempt status. This final step of filing Form 1023 is undertaken only after all preceding work is complete.

While each of the organizational steps outlined above began with work I started on my own, each document and system was ultimately the result of a cooperative effort and the shared expertise of collaborators. Once Mano a Mano's founding board was selected, it was closely involved in the start-up steps that followed.

## Lessons Learned During the Creation of Mano a Mano

*Be systematic and learn from the experiences of others.* Do your research. Board members, for example, may have relevant experience relating to not-for-profit status. They may have access to sample documents. But there are many other sources of valuable information and your efforts to seek them out will pay off.

*Begin as you mean to continue.* Carefully consider right from the start the focus and tenor you wish to establish for the organization.

*Recruit board members who provide expertise needed to create a well-functioning organization. Be clear about their time commitment and responsibilities.* One individual referred by a friend agreed to join the board because the request was clear and Segundo and I promised to respect her time.

*Focus organizational bylaws on board responsibilities and functions.* Do not try to define the organization's programs or operations in this document. The state of Minnesota requires that articles of incorporation and bylaws be filed with the secretary of state's office. If an organization changes either document, it must file the revised documents. Mano a Mano's bylaws focus on the authority, purpose, duties, meetings, and ethical conduct of the board. Because they do not attempt to define the organization's programs or its relationship with counterpart organizations in Bolivia, it has been necessary to change them only once—when economic development was added to the mission.

*Establish board policies* that define in more detail the expected conduct, responsibilities, and limitations of the board.

*Identify and address IRS reporting and regulatory requirements before creating internal processes* that might otherwise have to be undone or redrafted later.

*Keep detailed and accurate financial records.* Create them manually or with simple, user-friendly computer software. Choose software that can be expanded easily as the organization becomes more complex.

◆ ◆ ◆ ◆

Segundo and I did not start with the intention of creating a 501(c)(3) organization. Once we made the decision to do so, however, we never for a moment regretted it. We soon learned that forming a nonprofit enabled us to more effectively leverage surplus medical inventory in Minnesota to increase the capacity of health-care providers in Bolivia to serve impoverished patients. It also facilitated fundraising for that goal.

By 1996, Mano a Mano's third year, we had collected, processed, and shipped over 70,000 pounds of medical surplus to help address the health needs of impoverished Bolivians. The keys to achieving these results were a laser focus on the organization's mission; a strong social work and human rights philosophy that emphasized respect for and partnering with beneficiaries; a systematic gathering of information and planning of new tasks; endless hours contributed by Segundo, myself, and other dedicated volunteers; and flexibility to take advantage of unforeseen opportunities.

# 3

# Developing the Medical Supply Program

*Never doubt that a small group of thoughtful, committed citizens can change the world. Indeed, it is the only thing that ever has.*
**—Margaret Mead, renowned anthropologist[52]**

We started with a simple idea. We would collect never-used surplus medical supplies and lightly used medical equipment in Minnesota and make these items available to a hospital in Bolivia. Aware that medical services in Bolivia were rudimentary and that doctors lacked the most basic items, we wanted to transform items deemed useless here into articles useful for delivering medical services to those in need there.

Before seeking donations, we methodically analyzed every step of the workflow, from collection in Minnesota to patient use in Bolivia. In doing so, we worked backwards. It may seem counterintuitive, but we began at the end point in Bolivia to keep the focus on the beneficiaries. We wanted to ensure that everything we shipped to Bolivia was useful to local Bolivian health-care professionals and their patients. We started with on-site inquiries about priorities and estimated quantities needed.

We then worked back to the United States. We listed every task needed to get the required materials to their destinations. At each step we noted potential problems. While the following list is not an exact replica of the original, its structure and purpose are similar to the working template we created in 1994:

| Step | Potential Problem to Resolve; Task to Complete |
|------|-----------------------------------------------|
| 1. Health care professional uses item with patient | • Get needs list in order of importance<br>• Get staff and population size to understand quantity needed |
| 2. Health care facility distributes items to staff | • Ensure that an open review of distribution occurs in view of staff and public |
| 3. Health care facility receives items | • Create simple form for recording what is received<br>• Ask facility to post it in a public place for review |
| 4. Volunteers in Bolivia pick up items from customs | • Arrange method of transport from point of arrival to storage<br>• Arrange space for storage until all donations are distributed |
| 5. Obtain duty-free agreement from customs | • Seek contact within Bolivia who has authority to grant duty-free status |
| 6. Transport donated items to Bolivia | • Seek sources of free transport of cargo |
| 7. Store donated items in Minnesota | • Set aside space in home of founders |
| 8. Request donations from health care facilities in Minnesota | • List facilities in which friends and families work<br>• Prepare a letter that introduces Mano a Mano to potential sources<br>• Recruit volunteers to assist with contacts and with picking up donations |

| 9. Develop outreach to existing and potential donors | • Clearly define the message to potential donors, volunteers and the public in general<br>• Design a logo, letterhead and brochure |
|---|---|
| 10. Recruit volunteers | • Define process and assignments |
| 11. Seek funds | • Prepare letters and plan events |

# Setting Up Operation in Bolivia

A foremost concern at the outset was the integrity of our operation. A documented history of government and NGO corruption had been the downfall of many humanitarian efforts in Bolivia and elsewhere. We had heard the stories and read reports. We knew that bribery and extortion were treated as costs of doing business in some international transactions. We were determined Mano a Mano would not fall into that pattern. Segundo and I recognized that the most difficult steps in the process would occur in Bolivia. We paid meticulous attention to those junctures where corruption or the appearance of corruption might detract from our ability to serve those in need. To have any hope of long-term success, we knew Mano a Mano had to quickly establish and then maintain a reputation for integrity.

Another up-front concern was frugality. From the start, we resolved to do what we could ourselves and rely on generous friends to join us and form a volunteer force for good. We tenaciously stuck to the core principle that no funds would be squandered and nothing whatsoever would go to waste. We resolved to maximize the benefits that would find their way to doctors and patients in Bolivia.

### Step 1. Inventory of patient needs

Mano a Mano initially collected supplies and equipment for a medical group in Bolivia that is still operational but no longer affiliated with Mano a Mano. At the time of affiliation, the organization was a nonprofit thirty-two-bed hospital with a large outpatient clinic. Dr. José Velásquez, Segundo's brother and a founding member of Mano a Mano in Bolivia, was the director of the hospital and could guarantee that our donations would be used to serve the poor. This guarantee was crucial.

The group's target population comprised poor urban and peri-urban families who received care at a much lower fee than patients at private hospitals. As is true in most hospitals in the developing world, patients were expected to pay for their own treatment supplies. Families would typically scrape together their meager resources to meet their loved one's needs. With supplies donated from the United States, the medical group could treat these patients without requiring such extensive family sacrifice.

This early collaboration during Mano a Mano's Phase I (1994–96) created a win-win situation for both organizations. The medical group received supplies for its patients and equipment for its facility. In turn, its professional staff created an effective volunteer network to assist in completing the first four steps of our project: provide lists of most-needed items; ensure that the distribution of donations was transparent and documented; provide space for cargo storage upon its arrival in Bolivia; and pick up and transport the donated items to the health-care facility.

## Step 2. Ensuring that the distribution of donations was transparent and documented

Dedicated volunteers carried, loaded, and unloaded each item sent to Bolivia. The operation was orchestrated by Segundo's brother José, who found volunteers and supervised the group.

Bolivian volunteers recognized the need for and created a transparent system of inventory control. To avoid any suspicion of official or volunteer theft, they made a detailed record of every boxed item, presented the boxes along with the recorded lists to the health-facilities officials, unpacked the boxes in front of them with additional staff members present, and then posted the list on the wall for all to review. Lists were carefully maintained on site at the health-care facility and routinely shared with the Minnesota board of directors.

The lists served another purpose. They helped the medical group identify supplies and equipment beyond its needs. That identification process enabled the medical group to share excess supplies and equipment with government and other nonprofit hospitals, initiating a successful secondary distribution program that continues today.

The inventory control system underscored the importance of frugality. Even the smallest item was tracked and accounted for. Adherence to this inventory control system also sent a message. It signaled to the volunteer workforce that each step of Mano a Mano's operation was above board and free from corruption. To date, no person directly associated with Mano a Mano has ever been accused of taking any donated items for his or her own benefit.

**Step 3. Providing space for cargo storage in Bolivia**

Unloading items and moving them to storage was labor intensive. At the early stages of operation, it was an especially arduous task. The physical labor required of volunteers was complicated by a less-than-ideal storage space, which utilized a second floor. Every donated item had to be carried up and down steps. Volunteers used boards, logs, and brute force to lift and slide hospital beds, examination tables, and other heavy items to these temporary spaces until hospital rooms were ready.

**Step 4. Retrieval of shipments from customs and transportation to the health-care facility**

Shipments were transported by truck. Heavy lifting was also required at this stage, but that was the easy part. Interactions with customs agents were often more challenging—e.g., unnecessary delays, concerns that cargo might include expensive personal items for staff, proposed redirection of cargo to their warehouse, expectations of a bribe.

**Step 5. Obtaining the duty-free agreement with customs**

The most difficult step in the development of the medical donations program was obtaining the agreement for Mano a Mano medical cargo to enter Bolivia on a duty-free basis. Duty-free status was crucial to the program for two reasons. First, although all cargo was donated, customs charges duty fees based on an estimated purchase price, cost of shipping, and any other importing costs. Mano a Mano knew of another nonprofit organization that had been charged more than $40,000 to obtain and clear through customs one forty-foot container filled with medical supplies. It was an impossible sum for that fledgling organization and would have been for Mano a Mano as well. Second, the shipping program we began using in 1996 required that Mano a Mano obtain a duty-free agreement with the receiving country.

Through contacts with Bolivian nationals who lived in Minnesota, we identified an individual who worked for the Bolivian Interior Ministry, the office in charge of customs. Months of discussion with this contact, dozens of attempted telephone calls, and countless unsuccessful written requests proved fruitless and disheartening.

During this time we'd ignored a different customs-related lead because it hadn't seemed as promising as the approach to the ministry contact. We eventually turned to this alternative lead, eager for help and open to lessons. While we might have more efficiently achieved our goal without trial and error, this experience instilled an appreciation of the importance of flexibility and ability to recognize and pursue promising partnerships.

The U.S. Catholic Relief Services (CRS), a nonprofit located in Baltimore, had offered to assist Mano a Mano by bringing cargo into Bolivia under the auspices of its office in La Paz. Even after months of delay, their offer stood. The director agreed that Mano a Mano could send a detailed inventory of each shipment's contents to his agency, which would process the paperwork required by customs; receive the cargo; and turn it over to Mano a Mano. In return, CRS would receive items such as wheelchairs for use in its long-term care facilities. When we opened the formal letter of agreement between CRS and Mano a Mano, we cried with relief and deep gratitude for their generosity. CRS continued to act as our consignee until 2010, when Bolivian law regarding customs changed, requiring the consignee to complete extensive reports and related paperwork.

## Lessons Learned in Setting Up Operation in Bolivia (Steps 1–5)

*Begin with trusted relationships.* Mano a Mano developed because of the devotion and competence of trusted friends and family. As the circle grew, we never lost sight of the importance of trust, respect, and long-term relationships.

*Create a win-win situation.* Mano a Mano wanted to ensure that donations received by the organization would be used to treat needy patients. We did not have funds to pay staff or cover storage costs in Bolivia. The medical group we initially aligned with did not have sufficient funds to purchase medical supplies and upgraded hospital and clinic equipment, but did have usable storage space and staff who were willing to volunteer time.

*Stay in tune with the culture.* Volunteers recognized that Mano a Mano's reputation could be eroded by perceptions of corruption. They prevented future problems by setting up processes that were transparent and accountable.

*Be flexible and willing to forge new partnerships.* Obtaining a duty-free customs agreement was critical to the operation. When it was clear that obtaining an agreement specific to its organization wasn't feasible, Mano a Mano partnered with another organization that had the necessary agreement.

## Setting Up Operation in the United States

Domestic operations also required persistence, problem solving, and study. Our approach involved considerable trial and error.

### Step 6. Transporting donated items to Bolivia

As we set up operation in Minnesota, we began contacting air transporters. At that time, we thought in terms of a small number of items. We had in mind perhaps a few hundred pounds each year. We initially reached out to Northwest Airlines, Segundo's employer. Northwest did not fly to Bolivia, but agreed to transport Mano a Mano cargo free of charge to Miami. Segundo contacted Lloyd Aéreo Boliviano (LAB), the Bolivian airline, which agreed to a fifty percent discount in its charge from Miami to Bolivia. Having these agreements in place made it possible for Mano a Mano to move 1,500 pounds of medical surplus to Bolivia by mid-1995. However, the process was far from ideal.

Given the difficulties we encountered when shipping just boxes, Segundo knew it was essential to find an alternative shipper to transport the large items we hoped to acquire, such as hospital beds and cribs. The search for more adequate transportation failed to yield a viable lead until Segundo learned from coworkers that the National Air Guard sometimes trans-

## SEGUNDO'S ACCOUNT OF TRANSPORTING THIRTY-TWO BOXES OF SUPPLIES AS EXCESS BAGGAGE

We had packed over 1,500 pounds of supplies in boxes throughout the year. I planned to travel to Bolivia with them as soon as my vacation time arrived. I packed thirty-two boxes into the cheap little trailer that Joan and I had bought for donation pickups and strapped them down with bungee cords.

Moving these boxes in Miami was another story. I realized that they were delivered to the air cargo terminal at the other end of the airport. I had to figure out a way to transport thirty-two boxes from one terminal to the other. A taxi would not do. Not even a rental van would hold the thirty-two boxes. I took a taxi to air cargo, knowing that something would come up. No problem. But when I got there, I saw only loading docks and forty-foot truck trailers. I knew that none of these professional, semitrailer drivers would be willing to haul my boxes for just a few miles. While standing there searching for a solution, a *paisano* (a fellow Latino) appeared before me, driving a battered cattle truck. I knew he would help if asked, and he did. Together we loaded the boxes and hurried to the passenger terminal.

We had to unload on the outer median that divides several lanes of traffic from the airport itself. One by one, I moved boxes across two lanes of traffic to the terminal building and the Lloyd Aéreo Boliviano counter. All of the boxes arrived with me at the intended destination, our first successful shipment to Bolivia completed!

ported donated cargo from the United States to other countries. After six months of scouting, he traced these stories to their source. The U.S. State Department's Agency for International Development (USAID) and the Defense Department operated a joint program—the Denton Program—that authorized and arranged for military aircraft to transport humanitarian cargo to other countries on a space-available basis at no cost.

When we received the lengthy and complex application packet for this program, we learned that the maximum shipment was 100,000 pounds. At the time this vast number seemed laughable. We never imagined exceeding the maximum shipment. However, the program also specified a minimum shipment of 2,000 pounds. That was a concern. We wondered where and how we would come up with a large enough shipment to qualify for the program. Our concern was short-lived, however.

In 1996, Mano a Mano shipped our first Denton cargo; it weighed more than 37,000 pounds. As boxes kept coming out of the airplane, one of the Bolivian volunteers gasped and said, "They must have emptied out the whole United States." The Denton Program was incredibly important. Availability of military aircraft transport made it possible to ship large items, including examination tables, gurneys, and hospital beds. As a result, there was a dramatic increase in donations during year three.

Mano a Mano shipped all of our cargo—nearly two million pounds—through Denton until 2006, when we began to use USAID-funded container transport. Mano a Mano had the good fortune to ship all medical donations to Bolivia free of charge until 2011, a tremendous cost savings for a small organization.

The Denton process was extensive and required a detailed inventory of every item to be shipped. Fortunately, Mano a Mano had already created an inventory system to comply with IRS requirements. Our initial system was partially manual, with volunteers recording each item on their clipboard sheets as they packed. The data from the packing sheets was then later entered on a computerized spreadsheet. The paper system became more and more cumbersome as collections increased and more agencies began to request information about the inventory.

The State Department, to demonstrate the value of the Denton Program to Congress, requested paperwork to show the cost of medical supplies and equipment including the full value of items shipped. Customs in Bolivia wanted copies to ensure contraband items were not coming into the country duty free, and requested a minimal reference price for duty-free items. USAID inspectors, who opened a random selection of the boxes to ensure that their contents were correctly itemized and that no firearms were included, regularly wanted copies of inventory sheets. Container shippers needed inventory sheets to prepare a detailed bill of lading. Other nonprofit organizations who receive in-kind donations requested samples of our inventory documents. And potential donors, interested in more detail about the collections program, also requested lists of items shipped.

We found the paperwork somewhat onerous. Each requester wanted a different format. Many even required a different cost basis. Fortunately, though, our Minnesota volunteers were willing to do whatever it took to assure compliance with government requirements and responsive interaction with other entities.

When a volunteer offered to create an automated bar-code system, we jumped at the opportunity. It was an essential step. To implement the bar-code system it was necessary, however, to adapt our sorting and packing procedures to facilitate the transition. Under the new system we continued to divide cargo into twenty categories by type of medical supply—e.g., gloves, wound care, drapes, surgical instruments. We ordered preprinted labels with sequential numbers for each category. We placed the appropriate label on each box before sealing it, and then scanned the label bar code into the computer file. We weighed and measured the size of each box and immediately entered that data as well. Then we palletized the box and entered the pallet number into the computer file. With this new computerized system, customized reports became automated and at least this part of our lives became easier.

## Step 7. Storing donated items in Minnesota

Initial storage of donations designated for Bolivia was rudimentary at best. It all took place in and around our home. At an early stage we assumed Mano a Mano might collect about 1,500 pounds of supplies each year. We set aside space in a barn that had not been used for several years. It was a solid concrete block building with a cement floor. We designated one area of the barn for items that needed to be sorted and packed, and another area for packed boxes. During the cold Minnesota winters, loyal volunteers helped us carry everything that required sorting and packing into our finished basement. In the spring, we carried the packed boxes back up the stairs for storage in the barn.

As donations increased, they began to invade our home— first the garage and then the living room. To deal with the deluge, we moved the sorting process to the driveway during warm months. Soon we expanded the barn and put that new space into service. That too soon proved inadequate. By 1997 we began to store palletized boxes on our long driveway in all seasons, covering the pallets with tarps for protection against rain and snow. When yet more space was needed, we pitched three tents in the backyard. Using this ongoing process of improvisation, Mano a Mano stored its medical inventory free of charge until 2003. The potential hazards and deficiencies of such a ramshackle system were obvious.

Our zealous search for low-cost warehouse storage finally yielded results. A donor whose business had downsized offered ample warehouse space in a convenient location for substantially below-market rent. Mano a Mano accepted his offer and continued to use this space until we purchased our own facility in 2012.

### Step 8. Requesting donations from health-care facilities

Solicitations for surplus began with a brief introductory letter that we sent to a dozen health-care facilities thought to have large quantities of surplus. That letter paved the way for volunteers to request appointments to talk with a member of each facility's administrative staff. Volunteers actually given appointments arrived with a list of needed items. At first only one facility agreed to donate surplus items. All the others asserted that they did not have surplus items—that they essentially used everything. We went back to the drawing board, realizing that administrative personnel were the wrong targets.

What we came to understand was that administrators are not close enough to the situation. In addition, disposal of items treated as waste might have balance sheet implications and some administrators might worry that acknowledging "waste" at their facility could reflect poorly on them. With these thoughts in mind, we went another direction. The best sources, we decided, were nurses working on the floor, materials managers, and operating room staff. They are the people who know where the surplus is, what it is, and how to reserve it for later donation. By the end of year two, we had begun to tap into consistent sources of surplus.

Surplus occurs in health-care settings for various reasons. In conjunction with our requests for solicitations, we made it our business to figure out how and why surpluses occur.

- The medical system stresses efficient use of its professional staff's time. So supplies are packed into kits that include all items that the surgeon or other person performing a specified procedure is likely to need. Once the pack is opened, any unused items are discarded because the pack itself is now incomplete.

- When medical facilities change suppliers, they often dispose of items previously purchased from other suppliers.

- Occasionally facilities over-order a product. If the items occupy costly space and are not requested by staff, they may be discarded.

- Sometimes inexperience or misunderstanding results in an erroneous order.

- When health-care facilities remodel, there is a limited, or nonexistent, market for the items they have replaced.

- When medical facilities change décor, they often dispose of items that do not coordinate well with the new color scheme.

As we learned how to locate medical surplus, our level of donations increased quickly. By 1999 (year six), we were collecting 150,000 pounds annually.

Initially, Mano a Mano accepted all donations. Personnel in emergency rooms and surgical suites toss useful and expensive medical supplies into a Mano a Mano box. This is an obvious win-win for hospital staff reluctant to see supplies go to waste and for Bolivians trapped in poverty. Gradually we also started to amass gently used items from home-health agencies—braces, crutches, and wheelchairs. However, early in our organization's development, we had to draw a line when potential donors started bringing in used furniture, clothes, and toys. While these items could be put to good use in Bolivia, storage and transportation limitations highlighted the importance of closely adhering to our stated health-care mission.

## Step 9. Reaching out to existing and potential donors

An important part of Mano a Mano's initial success was ensuring that donors understood the impact their donations would have on the lives of poor Bolivians. Our conscientious outreach efforts to donors continue to the present.

From its earliest days, Mano a Mano has sent a brochure and a thank-you letter written on letterhead to every donor within one week of the donation. We personalize these letters by listing all donated items and explaining their significance to those who will receive them in Bolivia. Volunteers also meet with staff of each donating facility at least once a year to show them photos of their gifts being used in Bolivia.

To put our best foot forward and project the best image to our growing base of donors, we knew we needed to present a coordinated image. We collected brochures from many organizations and carefully examined their content. We wanted to design a logo that reflected the mission, the extreme need, a sense of organizational competence, and the organization's frugality. A volunteer designed a logo and letterhead using the simple design of two hands extended toward each other across the North and South American continents. On the recommendation of the director of another nonprofit organization, Mano a Mano registered a copyright for the logo. We continue to feature our original logo prominently in all literature, on the website, and even on T-shirts. Another volunteer contributed the tagline: "Putting surplus into service for better health."

## Step 10. Recruiting volunteers

Initially, Segundo picked up all of the medical donations himself. Later we simply asked family members and friends to assist in picking up donated items and in sorting and packing them. On a weekly basis, a group met in our home to sort and pack supplies. On Saturday mornings, volunteers met again to prepare equipment for shipment.

As donations increased and others began to join the volunteer groups, Mano a Mano decided to formalize its volunteer program. We began by purchasing liability insurance to cover volunteers when performing Mano a Mano tasks. Then we expanded our volunteer recruitment efforts. While word of mouth provided the primary source of new volunteers, we increased our outreach by recruiting volunteers from churches and local colleges. We created a sheet with emergency contact information for prospective volunteers to complete.

We interviewed all prospective volunteers about their interests and the organization's needs. While time consuming, those interviews yielded invaluable information that we might not have learned otherwise. For example, a volunteer whose initial interest was in collecting donated supplies eventually agreed to design the organization's first website.

We made sure volunteers had complete and accurate information about Mano a Mano and we attended to their comfort by scheduling breaks during work times and providing food and drink.

Sometimes we needed to intervene to prevent inappropriate behavior. During one packing session, a new male volunteer began to comment on how attractive a donated nurse's uniform would look on a young female volunteer. After a private conversation with the female volunteer about any discomfort she might have experienced, we quietly transferred the male volunteer to another assignment.

Another vital element is recognizing Mano a Mano volunteers. We created a set of postcards with Mano a Mano photos and mail them periodically with thank-you notes to our regular volunteers. We also host a volunteer picnic every summer, and honor an annual Volunteer of the Year with a special gift. For several years, Northwest Airlines donated tickets that were used for this purpose.

In 2000, a graduate student approached us with a proposal to travel to Bolivia to complete a research requirement, and asked for guidance on what she could study. Because volunteers completed all Mano a Mano work, we suggested she interview a sample of volunteers in both the United States and Bolivia about why they volunteer with the organization. She completed ten interviews in each country and elicited valuable information about why volunteers donated their time and what might cause them to stop volunteering. Although volunteers in the U.S. were on average fifteen years older than those in Bolivia, responses in both countries were nearly identical. People said they volunteered for two reasons: their commitment to Mano a Mano's mission, and their commitment to the organization's founders. They said they might stop volunteering if either changed.

*We wanted our Friday afternoon sort sessions to feel welcoming and support relationships among volunteers. So every week Joan and I would prepare bean dip, using a recipe created by one of the volunteers. Joan made hot cider on cold days and lemonade when it was warm. We always took a break together before folks had to leave. These were special times. We talked about what Mano a Mano was doing, what else we needed, and the general news from each of us. Volunteers looked forward to getting together and doing something they found meaningful every week.*

—Segundo Velásquez

## Step 11. Raising funds

Fundraising has been Mano a Mano's greatest ongoing challenge. Because this task is critical for all nonprofit organizations, a later chapter is devoted to the topic.

## Lessons Learned in Setting Up Operation in the United States (Steps 6–10)

*Analyze the workflow from beginning to end* before starting a program, and identify in detail all necessary tasks. Have confidence that each task is achievable. If we had doubted that our Bolivian founders would be able to complete their tasks in Bolivia, there would have been no point in collecting items in Minnesota.

*Begin small.* Mano a Mano had the opportunity to resolve issues that would have been insurmountable if the organization had been overwhelmed at the outset by a donation of 5,000 pounds. We wouldn't have known who would use it, how it would clear customs, or how to transport it.

*Keep good records.* Mano a Mano shipments could not have departed Minnesota or gained entry into Bolivia if the organization had not created clear and detailed records of all items transported. When in 2000 (year seven) Mano a Mano reached the income level at which an audit was required, its inventory system proved invaluable. The auditor required a listing of each item received and each item shipped, along with dates and dollar values. We hadn't anticipated an eventual need for audits of in-kind donations and were relieved to have nevertheless maintained the required information.

*Ask those who work in the health-care system where to find what you need.* Be sure to revisit potential donors to assure that those with incompatible agendas do not provide misinformation.

*Don't become a depository for things you don't need.* While it is tempting to take on additional donations, doing so can distract from the original mission. Set boundaries and stay true to them.

*Begin with simple written materials.* Having clear and persuasive literature in hand was essential for the many volunteers who made contacts with potential donors.

*Develop a clear, easy-to-communicate vision.* "Send medical donations to where they can save lives rather than to local landfills" and our tagline, "Putting surplus into service for better health" gave donors a clear, succinct message about our mission.

*Nurture, inspire, and recognize volunteers and donors.* People of goodwill are eager to give to a worthwhile project. Create a positive atmosphere and foster opportunities for interaction. We always provided snacks and drinks and made time to sit and talk with volunteers after completing tasks. By talking about Mano a Mano's work every week with volunteers while sorting supplies, and routinely updating donors about the impact of their donations, we fostered a strong sense of attachment to the organization. Remember to tell and show people you value their contributions to the organization.

*Respect volunteers' and donors' time.* To show respect for our volunteers' time, we organized tasks before they arrived and made sure that all needed packing materials were available. For health-care facility donors, we provided a conveniently placed donation box and accepted all discarded supplies.

◆ ◆ ◆ ◆

The medical supply program, Mano a Mano's longest-running program, remains fundamental to our operations. Minnesota volunteers collected medical surplus and their counterpart volunteers in Bolivia distributed those supplies to health-care professionals who served the very poor. Today most of the same Minnesota hospitals and clinics continue to donate excess supplies that are being put to use in Bolivia. Minnesota volunteers still gather on evenings and weekends to sort and inventory, and pack supplies for transport. Bolivian volunteers 4,623 miles away still gather to open boxes and sort medical supplies for distribution to local hospitals and distant clinics. There are currently around 400 Minnesota volunteers and 200 volunteers in Cochabamba.

As Mano a Mano approaches our twenty-year anniversary, we still rely on many of the systems we developed in our early days. At the twenty-year mark, we reflect with satisfaction on the adjustments and refinements we've made to cut costs, improve efficiency, comply with legal requirements, and work within a changing political climate. Our commitment to certain core principles—frugality, competence, and freedom from corruption—remains strong. As we move forward with this program and others, we count on the knowledge that our reputation for integrity precedes us.

# 4

# Building Clinics: The Model Emerges

*With adequate social opportunities, individuals can effective-*
*ly shape their own destiny and help each other. They need not*
*be seen primarily as passive recipients of the*
*benefits of cunning development programs.*
**—Amartya Sen, winner of the**
**1998 Nobel Prize in Economics[53]**

In its second phase (1997 to 2000), Mano a Mano evolved from an organization that shipped medical surplus to Bolivia to an organization that provided rural Bolivians with the opportunity to shape their own destinies. We made this remarkable leap by partnering with rural Bolivians to build health-care clinics in their communities.

By the end of Phase I in 1996, Mano a Mano had collected, processed, and shipped over 70,000 pounds of medical surplus to Bolivia. This surplus had reequipped Mano a Mano's initial Bolivian partner facility and allowed it to equip inpatient rooms in a thirty-two-bed hospital, ten outpatient examination rooms, a waiting room, surgical and delivery facilities, x-ray facilities, and a laboratory. The Bolivian partner now had on hand its own surplus of basic supplies. Given the bounty that was arriving from the United States, Mano a Mano volunteers in Bolivia began to share a sizable portion of the incoming cargo with other hospitals and clinics. These secondary donations increased the capacity of the Bolivian medical group and others to provide improved care to families who could not afford to pay, which clearly advanced Mano a Mano's organizational vision. Volunteers in both countries shared a strong sense of dedication to our mission and the belief that Mano a Mano was quickly emerging as a highly successful organization.

## Mano a Mano Initiates Two Community Clinics

Success with the medical surplus program led us to consider other ways Mano a Mano might work to improve health care in Bolivia. Board members familiar with the concept of satellite sites in underserved neighborhoods suggested establishing satellite clinics in poor barrios surrounding Cochabamba. When the Bolivian medical group expressed an interest in expansion, the Mano a Mano board resolved to build clinics in partnership with the medical group if the opportunity to fund the clinics arose.

The seventieth birthday of Gloria MacRae, a close friend and Mano a Mano volunteer, provided that opportunity. Celebrants raised $11,000, exceeding a goal of $4,000. Our astonished Bolivian volunteer counterparts decided to use the funds as seed money to build two satellite clinics—Clínica Gloria I and Clínica Gloria II. Thus began the Mano a Mano clinic program.

It is hard to overemphasize the importance of two critical points: organizational expansion must be mission-driven, and expansion requires additional resources. Mano a Mano's board

decided we would build a clinic in partnership with the Bolivian medical group if additional funding became available,
but we did not make a commitment to do so. Instead we took
advantage of serendipity, a one-time occasion that yielded substantial donations.

Once the Mano a Mano board gave its approval, Dr. José
Velásquez, the director of the medical group in Bolivia and Segundo's brother, immediately began to plan for an expansion
of the hospital's outpatient services. He focused on service to
dislocated miners who had moved to two villages in the mountains above Cochabamba. He traveled to the villages and talked
in person with villagers about his hospital and the services it
could offer them through the proposed community clinic. He
found they were eager to proceed. Mano a Mano volunteers in
Bolivia designed the clinic buildings. The villages donated land,
and villagers volunteered hundreds of hours of labor to complete construction. Mano a Mano funds helped pay for building
materials and skilled builders, and we donated all equipment
and supplies. In anticipation of the completion of construction
in 1997, José hired a physician and a nurse for each clinic. While
Mano a Mano was a key partner in their creation, these first two
clinics—Clínica Gloria I and Clínica Gloria II—belonged to the
medical group.

We collaborated closely with our counterpart founders in
Bolivia and communicated frequently with them. All of us were
committed to continuing the organization's culture of thoughtful planning, transparency, and frugality.

Unfortunately, we based our partnership with the Bolivian
medical organization on verbal agreements with individuals
rather than on written agreements regarding the organizations'
formal relationship. Although we informed Bolivian staff and
volunteers by letter of the medical items and funds that would
be provided and the purpose for which they could be used, we
did not request a reciprocal letter promising that these funds
and medical donations would indeed be used as intended. This

oversight later proved destructive.

The same year the Gloria clinics were completed, José was offered a position as director of a large teaching hospital in Cochabamba and he accepted. Mano a Mano's early success on the ground had depended in large part on José and his position as director at the medical group. When José left for his new position, Mano a Mano experienced immediate difficulties with his successor, who did not safeguard the previous values of transparency and frugality. Following this administrative change, Mano a Mano allocated a substantial amount of funds for the development of an infant and pediatric unit. However, it soon became clear that these funds had been misappropriated. Mano a Mano's board began to receive reports from the organization's staff that a significant amount of the budget had already been spent on lavish personal expenditures instead of the unit's construction, and volunteers feared that this specialized unit would not be created. When the organization's administrators failed to respond to requests for a report on the unit's progress, the Mano a Mano board discontinued its support. Within a few months, Mano a Mano severed the relationship with the medical group entirely and found itself in the midst of a crisis.

The medical group had provided volunteers, logistical support, and storage space in Bolivia. It also owned the Gloria clinics. We decided to use our modestly increasing funds for two pressing needs: to rent space in Bolivia that could be used to store and unpack medical donations and to hire a part-time employee to help distribute those supplies. José and several of his former colleagues continued to contribute countless volunteer hours to transporting, unpacking, and distributing medical donations.

## Lessons Learned in Constructing the First Two Clinics

*Institutions and their personnel are not synonymous.* Before sending equipment and funds for a new pediatric unit to Bolivia, we should have prepared a written agreement and required that it be signed by the organization instead of relying on verbal agreements. Lacking a written document, we had no legal means to retrieve donations when we concluded they were being misused. This unhappy experience reinforced the importance of trusted, long-term relationships and proceeding purposefully both when those connections are part of the dynamic and when they are not.

*Clinics must belong to the community* in which they are located, not to another organization. Although the Gloria clinics continue to provide health care to their communities, the villagers have little opportunity for input regarding the services they receive and no recourse when their needs are not met. All subsequent clinics belong to the communities that helped build them, giving them control of their health destiny.

## Creating the Mano a Mano Clinic Program

As medical donations increased, we became more and more concerned about our ability to make them available in rural areas. Over 60 percent of Bolivia's rural population has little or no access to health care. Rural rates of maternal, infant, and child mortality are much higher than those in urban areas. In spite of rural health statistics, most NGOs do not serve rural Bolivia.[54] Geographic dispersion of communities, transportation challenges, and language differences present formidable barriers. But we recognized the need and were determined to overcome the obstacles.

Our experience with the Gloria clinics demonstrated that Mano a Mano's Bolivian founders could successfully organize residents of impoverished communities to participate in planning and constructing a community clinic at very modest cost. This success led the board to set new goals related to clinic construction and staffing. We felt confident that the ongoing distribution of medical donations to a wider range of health-care programs would open doors in rural communities that would choose to collaborate with Mano a Mano in building community clinic facilities and programs.

In 1998, Mano a Mano volunteers in Bolivia received 120,000 pounds of medical surplus from the United States and constructed two more community clinics. Volunteers managed the increased demands on their time and resources, but couldn't continue at that pace while employed elsewhere on a full-time basis. The U.S. board decided that the organization could no longer expect to operate in Bolivia without paid staff and decided to fund two positions in Bolivia—one part-time position to direct the clinic projects and one full-time position to manage the increasing volume of medical inventory. Clinic budgets also included funds for one or two master carpenters.

## Establishing and Replicating the Clinic Development Model

Experience with the Gloria clinics helped Mano a Mano create a new model for bringing health care into impoverished communities. By the time four clinics were in full operation, most critical aspects of the model were well defined:

- **The community is central to the project.** Mano a Mano only works on projects requested by the community. Leaders must request a project. Residents must contribute the building site, local building materials, and all of the unskilled labor required to construct it.

- **The municipal government must contribute to the project.** The municipality makes a financial or in-kind contribution to construction. Over time, municipal officials and community leaders learn to co-administer the clinic with Mano a Mano.

- **All project participants must enter into a written agreement** that clearly delineates roles and responsibilities. (See the components of agreement below.)

## COMPONENTS OF AGREEMENT

| | |
|---|---|
| List of Parties to Agreement | Mano a Mano |
| Description of Parties | Municipality |
| Project Objectives | Community |
| Beneficiaries | Other Contributor |
| Project Description | Consequences of Non-Compliance |
| Specific Contributions | Signatures of all Parties |

- **Projects are implemented in Bolivia by Bolivians with U.S. board oversight.** Bolivians plan and build the clinic and co-manage its operation. The U.S. board provides financial and program oversight.

The Mano a Mano model is community-driven and built on strong partnerships with clearly defined accountability. It is implemented through careful attention to and execution of eight key steps.

### 1. Community requests and owns the project.

The story of how the first community-owned clinic was conceived and built illustrates the integral role of community in Mano a Mano's clinic program. In 1998 Mano a Mano volunteers were committed to seeking an opportunity to establish a rural clinic. When an equally determined midwife, Nora, requested supplies for her patients, the volunteers found the opportunity they sought. This summary of events was written by a Mano a Mano volunteer:

> For several years, Nora traveled the ninety miles from Cochabamba to her original home in Chullpa K'asa to deliver babies and bring medications. In 1997 she approached Mano a Mano volunteers, asking them to talk with Chullpa K'asa villagers about building a clinic there.
>
> When Mano a Mano's team first visited the village to discuss building a clinic, the town officials had already prepared information on what they would be able to contribute. But a vocal, skeptical member scoffed, "You're nothing but ch'amas (Quechua for noisemakers who promise everything but do nothing)!" He had often heard politicians make promises to his community, never to be seen or heard from again. José Velásquez challenged the listeners at that point, demonstrating that Mano a Mano had even brought the mold for adobes (mud bricks) so that residents could begin to make them. Cynicism began to give way to enthusiasm. Villagers said that, if they were to have a new clinic, it should be built with real city bricks, not the mud bricks used in the countryside. José countered that Mano a Mano would buy the bricks if residents could transport them.
>
> A resident who owned the only truck in town offered to haul the bricks if others would help pay for the cost of the fuel. Community residents in a single voice replied with their affirmations of willingness to help, and the partnership method was born. Three days later the truck and ten community members from Chullpa K'asa arrived in Cochabamba, eager to pick up the bricks for their new clinic. The truck returned home over the twisting, rocky roads—only ninety kilometers (around fifty-four miles), but a grueling six-hour trek over a

*16,000-foot pass. When the loaded truck could not reach the construction site, villagers grabbed their burden cloths, filled them with bricks and sand, and carried the heavy loads the last 200 yards on their backs.*

*When the Chullpa K'asa clinic opened in September 1998, the skeptic spoke passionately of Mano a Mano's staff and volunteers as the only dignitarios (dignitaries) who keep their promises. This leader continued by encouraging his compañeros (companions) to use clinic services, adding with conviction, "Now our wives and children won't die."*

## 2. Conversations between Mano a Mano and community members clarify the project.

Each clinic has its own story. Leaders from Tablas Monte, a village perched on a Cochabamba Valley mountainside, requested a clinic for the village in a late-night visit to José. The determination of these *campesinos* (country people) persuaded José to consider building a clinic in their community. Mano a Mano volunteers proceeded to the next step—conversations with the community. They toured the village, noting its size, economic base, and available resources (such as sand). They held meetings to document local needs, explained what would be required of the community to complete a clinic project, and assessed residents' motivation to work on it. Community residents participated in all aspects of planning and construction of their clinic.

Mano a Mano works with community residents as full partners, always beginning with the assumption that they are capable, motivated individuals who simply lack the material and educational resources required to improve their circumstances. For example, in the case of the Chullpa K'asa clinic, Mano a Mano deferred to the wisdom of the community in electing to use long-lasting commercial bricks rather than inexpensive, locally-formed adobe bricks.

## 3. Government entities become partners who enable and help sustain the project.

Partnerships with both the municipal government and the Bolivian Ministry of Health's Regional District are critical to ensure all clinics' long-term sustainability. Mano a Mano requires that municipalities, roughly equivalent to a county in the United States, become formal project partners. Community members must obtain their municipal officials' formal commitment to play an active role in the project. That role must include both a financial or in-kind contribution to clinic construction and agreement to co-administer the clinic along with community leaders and Mano a Mano within three years of clinic opening. As co-administrator, the municipal office bills the Ministry of Health for reimbursements, co-manages reimbursement funds and patient fees along with clinic staff, and continues to pay any staff salary for which it accepted responsibility in the partnership agreement. The patient fees and the reimbursements finance the ongoing operation of the clinic.

Mano a Mano clinics become the official provider of health services within designated geographic areas. The Bolivian Ministry of Health's Regional District defines clinic goals and reimburses clinics for all pre- and postnatal clinic visits, deliveries, services for children up to age five, and the diagnosis and management of diseases such as tuberculosis. It also provides age-appropriate vaccines for women and children, rabies vaccines for animals, and posters with pictures that provide health information.

The Mano a Mano clinic development model taps into all available resources. While the Bolivian Ministry of Health has minimal funds available for clinic construction, it does have available funds for staff salaries and reimbursement for care provided. This has led to Mano a Mano designing, building, and co-administering clinics while relying heavily on the ministry to fund ongoing care.

In Phase III (2001–04), the ministry began to pay for at least one staff salary in most Mano a Mano clinics through a permanent line item in its budget. With recognition of the vital role these clinics play, over the years the ministry increased its financial stake in clinics' continued operation. Currently, the ministry funds the salaries of eighty-one percent of Mano a Mano clinic staff members, while municipal governments and other Bolivian sources cover the remainder. Mano a Mano now pays no portion of staff salaries. This arrangement capitalizes on the ability of the Bolivian government to pay doctors and nurses who serve the rural population, and allows Mano a Mano to concentrate its resources on new clinic construction.

Health district staff members have expressed astonishment at the quality and size of Mano a Mano's clinics given their modest cost. Mano a Mano budgeted $12,000 to construct each of its first six 1,400-square-foot, brick-and-cement clinics, including costs for running water, indoor plumbing, and electricity. By contrast, the ministry was budgeting $10,000 (U.S.) just to repair its adobe constructions with no budget for new construction. Villagers often remark that Mano a Mano is the only organization to come into their communities, keep its word, and complete projects without a hint of corruption.

### 4. Formal agreements define the project.

Before any building begins, elected community leaders, municipal officials, and Mano a Mano representatives clearly define and agree upon each participating entity's responsibilities. Mano a Mano prepares a written agreement to be read and signed in a public ceremony. Thus, each community and its municipal officials publicly demonstrate their willingness to be full partners with Mano a Mano in building and operating the clinic. Once the agreement is signed, Mano a Mano holds all partners accountable to deliver on their obligations. On one occasion, Mano a Mano temporarily closed a clinic when the elected officials defaulted on their obligations. Elected officials then rectified the problem.

The community generally provides: the land for its clinic, any locally available building materials (e.g., sand, gravel, stone), and all unskilled labor required during the construction process (e.g., clearing brush and debris, transporting water to bricklayers, carrying hand tools and materials to builders). Mano a Mano provides: the bulk of the building materials, the services of skilled master builders, and transportation of personnel and materials to the building site. Upon completion of construction, Mano a Mano equips and supplies the clinic. The municipality makes a financial contribution to the project; may purchase a portion of the furnishings; and connects the center to electricity, if available. Construction usually takes about four months.

## HOLDING THE MUNICIPALITY OF CAMPO VÍA TO ITS PARTNERSHIP AGREEMENT

When José learned that the Campo Vía clinic nurse had not received her first salary payment, he immediately called the office of the mayor who had made a commitment to fund this position. Following up one week later, he learned that, despite the mayor's promise, the nurse still had not been paid. José talked with Segundo and me about possible solutions. We all agreed there was a calculated risk with any approach. If they shut down the clinic to force payment and the municipality didn't pay, we would have to explain the project failure to funders. On the other hand, not closing the clinic could make it impossible for Mano a Mano to hold municipalities to their agreements in the future. We agreed with José's recommendation to close the clinic.

José drove to Campo Vía, explained to villagers that the mayor had failed to pay the nurse, and very publicly locked the clinic. In response, the villagers jumped into the back of a local cattle truck, drove to the mayor's office, and refused to leave until the nurse was paid. Their loud protest met with success. The nurse received her salary and the clinic reopened.

Broad-based participation and signed agreements ensure the soundness and continued viability of each clinic. Just as important as the sense of ownership and legal protection, these elements give communities a sense of entitlement that extends beyond the right to receive basic medical care. As members of marginalized communities become aware of and gain rights pertaining to their own health care, they become empowered to pursue their rights in other areas.

## 5. Mano a Mano leads the partnership to implement the project.

Each step of a clinic-building project provides Mano a Mano with an opportunity to stimulate community cohesion, reinforcing for villagers a sense of ownership of and responsibility for the clinic. Mano a Mano works with community councils on methods for recruiting and scheduling villagers to contribute the unskilled labor required to build their clinic. Communities are also encouraged to create their own approaches. Generally, councils expect that all able-bodied adolescents and adults participate in the volunteer pool. Every day, four to five members of the volunteer pool work alongside Mano a Mano's master builders until the project is completed.

Some communities devise other volunteer scheduling methods that work better for them. In one project, villagers decided to each contribute two pesos (thirty cents) to pay two of their neighbors to work nearly full time on the clinic, learn about all aspects of the construction, and then teach the skills to other villagers. In another village, residents and clinic staff agreed that the clinic would provide a free medical examination in return for a specified number of extra hours worked.

Because machinery and electricity are not usually available, builders and volunteers complete all construction work by hand. Builders lay cement and bricks, construct interior walls, tile the floors, and install the plumbing. Volunteers work alongside them, clearing brush and rock from the site, carrying pails of water for mortar, sifting sand through a screen, and mixing cement in a wheelbarrow or fifty-gallon barrel turned by hand. Together they lift the roof timbers with pulleys and ropes. And, when they finish, the community celebrates its clinic with pride and gratitude.

After Mano a Mano began to construct clinics in remote rural areas, it faced an unforeseen obstacle: how to best recruit committed health-care professionals to these areas and retain them. Communities had brand new health-care clinics, but available housing was often substandard. The only potential housing for health-care professionals was a one- or two-room adobe dwelling with dirt floors and thatched or tin roofs.

Mano a Mano decided to incorporate living quarters into future clinics, and subsequently added living quarters onto the very early clinics that did not have them. These quarters include a bedroom for the physician, a bedroom for the nurse, a living room, a small kitchen, and a bathroom. These rooms are not used by patients. Having on-site housing for staff also provides the advantage of essentially having care available on a twenty-four-hour basis. This decision proved to be remarkably successful. Excellent living quarters, a clean and functional clinic, and the availability of medical equipment and supplies create an environment in which medical personnel can provide high-quality care. Since adding living quarters to the clinics, Mano a Mano has had no difficulty finding or retaining staff.

Throughout the construction phase, Mano a Mano's central office remains in contact with the construction site via two-way radio. Only rarely do rural communities have any restaurant or lodging facilities. This means that the four or five master builders employed by Mano a Mano live in the community for the duration of the project. Community volunteers prepare food for the builders and all other volunteers working on the project on any given day.

Mano a Mano purchases building materials in bulk and calculates to the last brick and door knob what materials must be sent to the building site. It hires trucks to haul its first shipment of materials, i.e., everything needed to complete structural work. When this work nears completion, the office sends the second shipment of materials to finish all construction, i.e., plumbing supplies and electrical wiring, if electricity is available. Staff members inspect a clinic at least twice—once during construction and again upon completion—to ensure that it meets specifications.

The weekend before a clinic opening, Mano a Mano volunteers travel from Cochabamba with all of the medical supplies, equipment, and furnishings. Together with community volunteers, they clean the clinic and move in everything from examination tables and hospital beds to packages of needles and gauze. They hang curtains, make the beds, and drape ribbon across the front entrance for the ceremony. Most of the medical equipment and supplies come from the inventory of medical surplus sent from Minnesota.

## 6. All partners participate in opening the project.

Bolivian communities always plan large and colorful opening

fiestas. When clinics open, *everyone* attends—from children dancing in the street in traditional costumes to the village elders admiring the windows and real bricks in the building to infants with a flair for a dramatic entrance.

The clinic in the town of Japo (population 9,700), which is about eighty-five miles from Cochabamba, took about four months to build and was completed in 2003. Japo resident Paulina was sad to think that she would be the only one of her friends and family to miss the clinic's grand opening celebration. So, despite being nine months pregnant, she walked the whole way to the clinic site. Perhaps it was the heat, the walk, or the excitement; whatever the cause, when the first dignitary launched into his speech, Paulina felt her first contraction. Moments later, her water broke and clinic staff rushed into action. They scurried to get Paulina set up in a room and ready to deliver her baby. The clinic, it seemed, had its first patient.

Throughout the delivery, Paulina listened to the sound of applause, cheers, and music that drifted in through an open window. She wasn't sure if the dignitaries, school kids, and Mano a Mano staff stretched their speeches and songs to stall for her benefit or if the celebration just naturally takes hours. In any event, Paulina had time to safely deliver her little boy, and the clinic staff had time to tidy her room for the grand opening tour. Having a mother and her tiny newborn essentially on display was a first for Mano a Mano and certainly a memorable first for Paulina and her son.

## 7. Clinic staff initiates project services.

The Bolivian Ministry of Health sets goals for all health-care facilities that receive its funds—goals for a percentage of area children who receive vaccinations, for pre- and postnatal care, and for the management of chronic diseases. To meet these goals and accomplish other health-care objectives, Mano a Mano has established certain protocols that cover the basic services each clinic provides:

- Community organization and outreach to inform community residents about clinic services and encourage their use

- Preventive services, including child and adult vaccinations, health education, well-child visits, family planning, prenatal and postnatal care

- Deliveries attended by trained medical staff

- Acute care for illness and accident cases

- Management of illnesses such as tuberculosis

Up to ten community residents are trained as volunteer health promoters who support the professional staff. They do so by promoting use of the clinic to their neighbors; performing first aid; assisting the medical staff to teach sanitation, nutrition, and basic childhood milestones; and stressing the importance of vaccinations, prenatal care, and deliveries attended by clinic personnel.

Mano a Mano systematically addresses any serious barriers to medical staff retention. By constructing cement and brick buildings that are easy to clean and maintain, incorporating living quarters for staff into its clinics, ensuring that clinics are well-equipped and supplied on a regular basis, and providing ongoing supervision and training for professional staff, Mano a Mano has successfully recruited and retained a cadre of competent, dedicated professionals to staff our rural clinics. Doctors and nurses view the clinics, the private apartments, the medical supply system, and the association with a network of medical professionals as invaluable benefits.

Work in a rural clinic inevitably presents many unavoidable challenges. For example, each clinic plans vaccination campaigns against childhood diseases in collaboration with the Bolivian Ministry of Health, which involve walking from house to house throughout the community, administering age-appropriate vaccinations, and recording them. This trek often requires climbing mountains, crossing small rivers on foot, and walking very long distances. The following excerpt from the journal of Dr. Silvia Condori illustrates what is typical for doctors working for Mano a Mano clinics in rural Bolivia:

> *My God, the things I have seen in this place! As a medical student, I always promised myself that I would do anything to save the life of a patient. How naïve I was. My first trip out of this village was to Sumala. They told me it was a long walk, but I never imagined how long. We walked for twelve hours without a rest, and then slept by the side of the path. In some places you have to climb along rocks overlooking the river, hanging on to avoid falling in. I arrived in Sumala dripping wet without a change of clothes, which is how I attended to patients waiting for me. On the way back, I attended to a pregnant woman in her home who was fine. She gave no sign that in a few hours she would be in a desperate state. After I arrived in the clinic the next day her husband came running in, saying she had fallen during the night. Her water had broken, she was hemorrhaging and feverish. Her husband said he and other villagers could carry her on a litter as far as Sonoma (a distance of fifty kilometers) where the ambulance could meet her. I got a ride to Sonoma on a truck, met the patient there, and rode with her in the ambulance to the hospital in Tarabuco. Thank God, she delivered a healthy baby. And that was just the first of my patients today.*

Mano a Mano's clinic staff members show great devotion to caring for patients in extremely difficult circumstances. Dr. Condori's brief account speaks to the daily challenges doctors face. On the day in question, she traveled more than thirty-one miles by truck over rough terrain. When Mano a Mano hires physicians, it seeks those as dedicated as Dr. Condori to saving the lives of their patients.

## 8. Mano a Mano's Cochabamba office develops human resources.

We recognize that sturdy buildings, excellent supplies, and clean living quarters alone do not constitute health care. It is the medical staff and their commitment that matters most to the villagers. It is critically important to increase staff capacity, particularly in rural areas in which no other professional resources exist. With this in mind, Mano a Mano invests significant resources to train and advise each clinic's medical staff, volunteer health promoters, and community councils. Mano a Mano offers ongoing supervision and continuing medical education to clinic physicians and nurses. We want to ensure that best medical practices are applied and create an incentive for staff to serve in remote rural villages.

Mano a Mano contacts each clinic staff member via short-wave radio every day during his or her first year and at least weekly in subsequent years. In addition, the supervising physician from the Cochabamba office provides on-site supervision and training on a quarterly basis during the first year, with annual visits once a new doctor has gained some experience. Among geographically dispersed personnel, this ongoing contact creates confidence, cohesion, and a strong sense of belonging to Mano a Mano. Clinic staff often cites this sense of being "part of the family" as one of their reasons for applying for a Mano a Mano position and then continuing to work in isolated areas to provide the best possible care for patients.

Each year, medical staff members from Mano a Mano clinics attend at least one three-day workshop that is organized by Mano a Mano's Cochabamba staff and presented in the city. Topics generally focus on attendees' immediate concerns.

Traumatology, nutrition, biosecurity, problem pregnancies, and family violence appeared on a recent list. Many faculty members from the Cochabamba medical school have taught continuing education classes for Mano a Mano clinic staff on a pro bono basis.

In 2009, Mano a Mano developed its first International Acute Care Conference in collaboration with volunteer doctors and nurses from Medical Educators for Latin America (MELA) in Minnesota. A weeklong conference in April 2009 focused on traumatology and included many opportunities for hands-on demonstrations. Twelve health-care professionals traveled to Bolivia from St. Paul to present this conference. It was wildly successful. Word of the unique opportunity spread quickly throughout the Cochabamba area. Health-care professionals from outside the Mano a Mano network requested permission to attend future conferences.

Minnesota health-care professionals who participated were profoundly touched by the experience and decided to present another conference in December 2009. Held in the auditorium of a large hospital, the December conference drew over 300 participants, including health-care personnel who do not work in Mano a Mano settings. Now these conferences occur annually, with Minnesota hospital staff applying to MELA for the opportunity to spend a week of their vacation time and their own funds to train their Bolivian counterparts alongside Mano a Mano.

Mano a Mano's continuing education program is unparalleled in Bolivia. Bolivian staff members work in extraordinarily difficult circumstances to provide quality health care to the hundreds of thousands of patients they serve. Medical personnel attribute their successes to Mano a Mano's supervision of their work and the ongoing education Mano a Mano provides. Evaluation questionnaires completed by workshop participants consistently show that over 90 percent of respondents consider the workshops to be of high value in their clinic practice.

Community volunteers who are recruited as health promoters receive training and materials from the Mano a Mano supervising physician. Course content includes first aid, sanitation, nutrition, basic childhood milestones, the importance of vaccinations for children, the necessity of prenatal care, the advantages of giving birth at the clinic, and an overview of clinic services. Health promoters are community members selected by community leaders. They have proven their dedication to improving lives in their villages through participation in the clinic building process. Because they are members of the communities they serve, health promoters are fully immersed in the culture and speak the languages of their communities. Their knowledge and sensitivity lead to wider acceptance of the clinic services by others in the community.

Health promoters use pictures to illustrate basics such as boiling water, burying trash, and proper bathroom use. Parents are taught to recognize developmental progress, how to know when their children are sick, and how to remedy some of the most common ailments. Parents are also taught techniques for limiting the spread of contagious diseases. Pregnant women learn about the advantages of prenatal care and giving birth in a clinic or in the home with medical staff present. Health promoters, working with clinic staff and school personnel, take responsibility for teaching both children and adults the importance of using the sanitary facilities that Mano a Mano helped construct.

Mano a Mano staff credit health promoters with saving lives in clinic communities. The Cochabamba office's supervising physician describes the close working relationship between the physicians and health promoters in responding to emergencies:

*A young woman who lives about a nineteen-hour walk from Colonia Andina had recently heard about the clinic from her husband's labor sindicato (union). She had many problems when her first baby was born and decided when labor began*

75

*that she would try to get to the clinic so the doctor could deliver this baby. She and her husband started out with the woman riding their burro. They had traveled for about fifteen hours when the women said she simply could not go on. The husband rushed to the clinic and Dr. Guevara and one of the promoters got on the clinic's motorcycle and followed him to the path where he had left his wife to rest. When they arrived, the baby had been born but had scrapes and cuts on his head that were already showing signs of infection. The mother was bleeding and the placenta had not been delivered. The doctor cared for the mother while the promoter cleaned the baby and dressed his cuts. The family spent the next week in the clinic and then returned home with a healthy mom and baby.*

Rural Bolivian communities govern themselves through locally elected councils—the *Junta Vecinal*. Through these councils, communities initiate requests for clinics. Mano a Mano helps them organize themselves and the larger community to participate in all aspects of planning and construction. The councils form an integral part of the process, beginning with the negotiation of the formal agreement with Mano a Mano.

Mano a Mano staff engages councils in making decisions regarding clinic operations and teaches them about administration, financing the clinic, and speaking out for increased access to government services. Although national legislation requires that municipalities allocate a portion of their taxes to health care, many rural residents are unaware of this requirement. Mano a Mano informs communities of their rights and responsibilities regarding health care and mobilizes communities to advocate that tax revenues be spent as directed. Given their considerable investment of labor and devotion, community residents are strongly motivated to learn to maintain their clinics and ensure they provide quality health care over the long term.

# Lessons Learned in Establishing and Replicating the Clinic Development Model

*Be community-driven.* Members of the community, the direct beneficiaries, must care enough about their clinic project to ensure that it continues to function well.

*Plan from the ground up.* Use the knowledge and skills of those who live every day with the challenges and are best equipped to manage and resolve them.

*Begin with a manageable pilot project.* Resolve issues on a small scale before they become costly.

*Leverage strong partnerships* to ensure sustainability.

*Establish a contract between partners that clearly delineates roles and responsibilities.*

*Construct buildings of excellent quality.* The insistence of Chullpa K'asa residents that their clinic be constructed of "real city bricks," not adobe, led to a decision that all future clinics would be of brick construction and built to last for decades.

*Include in-clinic living quarters for medical staff.* This helps address an important barrier to attracting and retaining high-quality medical staff.

*Give clinic personnel the support they need to provide superior care.* Mano a Mano maintains at least weekly contact via two-way radio and yearly supervisory visits with clinic staff. Medical staff members attend continuing education workshops that Mano a Mano offers every month in Cochabamba. In addition, up to ten community members are trained as volunteer health promoters to aid the medical staff.

From the beginning, Mano a Mano intentionally developed programs that engage rural residents as full and equal partners. Under the community model, Mano a Mano supplies the material resources that rural communities lack. During the construction phase, Mano a Mano's carpenters work with villagers to construct a sturdy brick structure built to last. After a project is completed, rural residents serve as indispensable team members in the health-care delivery system. The clinic development model requires that the community itself own the clinic and participate as an essential and equal partner in planning, building, maintenance, and management. This development model provides opportunities for community members to shape their own collective destiny and help each other.

# 5

# Building Infrastructure to Accelerate Growth in the Community Clinic Program

*Before everything else, getting ready is the secret of success.*
—Attributed to Henry Ford, founder of Ford Motor Company

By the end of 2000, Mano a Mano was typically collecting more than 200,000 pounds of medical surplus each year, easily enough to supply and equip its seven community health clinics and to fill requests from more than one hundred other health organizations serving the poor. We couldn't pause to admire how far we'd come when so much remained to be done, however. Dozens of rural communities had approached Mano a Mano with clinic requests that could not be filled for lack of funds. We began to seek other opportunities to raise the money needed to expand the clinic program. The results of this effort ushered in a new phase of dramatic growth, Phase III, from 2001 to 2004. This phase, more than any other, exceeded our expectations. It began with a comprehensive effort aimed at getting ready.

## Seeking Funds to Expand the Clinic Program

In March 2000, the Mano a Mano board decided to offer a guided trip to Bolivia as a fundraising effort. Participants would visit Mano a Mano projects and travel through the countryside. The intent was twofold: to raise funds through the trip fee, and to interest travelers in supporting Mano a Mano on an ongoing basis. We asked a travel agent with experience in Latin American travel to organize a ten-day trip that would include popular tourist sites and the opportunity to see Mano a Mano projects firsthand. Nine people with a strong interest in Mano a Mano joined. They took part in a televised distribution of wheelchairs to severely disabled individuals and visited the Mano a Mano clinics. The group's small size made it possible for them to interact personally with patients and staff.

One traveler, who eventually became known to Mano a Mano as our anonymous donor contact, returned home impressed and helped us obtain a planning grant to develop a funding proposal for multiple clinics. That grant made it possible for José Velásquez to travel to Minnesota and spend a month with his brother Segundo and me. Together the three of us agreed upon the details of the community clinic model; designed a seven-year plan for thirty clinics and a fourteen-year plan for eighty clinics; and calculated budgets for both options. These final proposals were based on the existing clinic development model that had been improved upon through four years of piloting one clinic project at a time. We hammered out the complexities of constructing clinics, bringing them into full operation, and continuing to support those clinics through the medical distribution program. The proposal detailed every budget line item. It included the points at which to add staff positions and purchase equipment and vehicles. It set out what salaries would be paid to a physician and nurse for each new clinic.

It was during this planning process that Segundo, José, and I made one critical change to the model. To fund clinic network expansion at the pace of six new clinics each year for five years, we decided to require that a Bolivian funding source pay the salary of one of the clinic staff from the day of hire. We also stipulated that Bolivian sources, primarily the municipalities and the Bolivian Ministry of Health, assume responsibility for both staff salaries within three years of clinic opening. This was not a casual decision. It was based on a thorough under-standing of public project financing in Bolivia, a clear sense of the capacity of government entities, and in-depth knowledge of cultural norms and differences. We knew we were asking more than anyone had before of these governmental entities, but we also recognized that if Mano a Mano took ongoing re-sponsibility for both staff positions in each clinic, the funding burden would hamper our ability to expand the program to more communities.

Our anonymous donor contact arranged for the donor and his attorney to meet with José, Segundo, and me. As we pre-pared for what could be a life-changing meeting, we learned of a dramatic shift in the donor's circumstances and therefore our prospects. A few days prior to the scheduled meeting date, we were informed that the anonymous donor had suffered a heart attack followed by a severe stroke and was in critical condition. We assumed that our request would be set aside.

We learned that we were not the only people blessed with a determined spirit. The anonymous donor and his wife decided that a meeting should still occur at which she would speak for both of them. Aware that this woman's thoughts were tied to the constant flurry of activity in an intensive care hospital room, each Mano a Mano representative spoke in turn about portions of the proposal and then answered questions. After two hours, the donor's wife shoved her copy of the proposal across the table to her attorney and said, "Make it happen." The anonymous donor approved our thirty-clinic proposal with the understanding that Mano a Mano would request funding for another fifty clinics if the project succeeded. We had four months to prepare for the launch of a thirty-clinic project.

## Setting Up Infrastructure for the Thirty-Clinic Project

Although the anonymous donor required that 100 percent of grant funds be transferred to Bolivia, the fiduciary responsibility for these funds remained with the U.S. board of directors. The IRS specifically requires that a U.S.-based organization that funds programs in other countries not function merely as a pass-through. The U.S. organization must play a significant role in developing and monitoring the implementation of projects and must retain ultimate control of the use of any funds raised in the United States. An organization that does not meet these requirements may lose its nonprofit status.

*Mano a Mano Bolivia.* During Mano a Mano's first five years of operation (1994–99), a Bolivian steering team of dedicated medical professionals had volunteered their time to oversee the projects there. When Mano a Mano severed its relationship with the medical group with which it had initially collaborated, we recognized that we needed to create an entity we could trust. So we created a new nonprofit organization in Bolivia to continue to carry out the work of Mano a Mano.

In 1999, Mano a Mano Bolivia incorporated as an NGO under Bolivian law. As such, it had full authority to respond to requests for assistance, design its own projects, establish its own work processes, and spend funds raised in the United States in accordance with U.S. law, donor designations, and guidelines established by the Mano a Mano U.S. board. As

Mano a Mano U.S. undertook preparations for the thirty-clin-ic project, we worked in close partnership with Mano a Mano Bolivia. Consistent with legal requirements, the two entities set up cooperative systems to monitor and control the dispersal of program funds.

To plan and prepare for the clinic project, three Mano a Mano Bolivia board members traveled to the United States to meet with Segundo and me. We spent three weeks togeth-er, working to address and define internal procedures for the management of Bolivian bank accounts, accounting protocols, reporting requirements, hiring of staff, and vehicle purchases. This group also defined the method for transferring and track-ing funds sent from Mano a Mano U.S. to Mano a Mano Bolivia.

These joint meetings were critical not only for the practical problems the group confronted together but also as a way to build trust, a vital intangible element of our ongoing collabora-tion. The group met daily for six to eight hours, taking time to ensure that each participant understood the others' viewpoints and concerns. Cross-national and cross-cultural understand-ing became more challenging and extremely critical as Mano a Mano prepared for a dramatic increase in program scope. With-out focus and dedication to the mission, a problematic dynamic or communication breakdown could have derailed our efforts. We moved forward, realizing that all areas of conflict had to be addressed, respected, and dealt with for a project of the scale we now envisioned to succeed. Moving forward has not always been easy, but we all agreed that this extraordinary opportunity to serve Bolivia's poor had to rise above any cultural conflicts, and we all committed to putting the mission first.

*Banking and accounting.* First, the group reviewed the banking systems in the United States and Bolivia. We raised certain fun-damental questions: What legal documents and processes are necessary in order to open a Bolivian bank account? Who has legal authority to open accounts? What fees do banks charge for each type of account and service? Whose signatures are required for checks and wire transfers? How long does it take for transferred funds to be deposited in the destination account? What are the interest rates for varying types of accounts? What types of report does the bank generate for its customers? If the bank fails, is the account protected or guaranteed?

Up to this point, Mano a Mano U.S. had transferred sums of up to $15,000 to Mano a Mano's team in Bolivia two to four times yearly. Both the Mano a Mano U.S. and Bolivian organizations understood regulations and fees in both countries well enough to manage the modest funds that supported its programs. Both had simple computerized accounting systems that generated all reports needed for internal review and yearly audits in the United States. During Phases I and II, a Minnesota bank used its standard procedure for wire transfers to send the designated amount to a bank account in Cochabamba registered in the names of three Mano a Mano volunteers, all of whom signed for withdrawals.

As the group prepared to manage much larger sums, we revisited all aspects of banking and accounting practices. Each point required hours of discussion to ensure everyone understood the implications of decisions for Mano a Mano in both countries. The group approached each point by reviewing, step-by-step, the processes used by banks in each country. For example, a customer in Bolivia might wait in several different lines for an entire day to complete a transaction that could be accomplished in Minnesota within a few minutes. In Minnesota, a customer could transfer funds between a savings account and a checking account with a phone call at no charge. A similar transfer could cost several hundred dollars and take several hours in Bolivia. Reviewing the details helped us recognize and take into consideration the time required for Bolivians to complete seemingly simple tasks.

We were sometimes confounded by the intricacies of the discussions, but everyone at the table recognized the importance of getting this right. The nuances of financial transactions in developing countries need to be addressed and understood by any group that hopes to undertake a similar project. These Bolivian examples only hint at the complex differences:

- To open a bank account in Bolivia, a business must conform to an extensive set of regulations regarding taxes, and all Bolivian nonprofits must meet those same requirements. Taxes include sales tax on any purchase for which the buyer receives a receipt, and for any service for which it receives payment. It often takes years to obtain the requisite permits and approvals. Because Mano a Mano Bolivia did not initially meet these myriad tax-related requirements, the organization could not open an account in its own name. Consequently, we decided that no business account would be opened and that instead funds would be deposited into a new personal account in the name of the executive director, the accountant, and one other board member. All three signatures would be required to withdraw any funds.

- Funds deposited in Bolivian banks are not guaranteed by the national government or any other entity. Given this concern, we decided to hold all funds in the United States until shortly before they were needed for Bolivia projects. Doing so was deemed the safest alternative.

- The high cost of banking transactions in Bolivia affected decisions regarding how and when to transfer funds from the United States. While Minnesota banks charge thirty dollars to transfer an unlimited dollar amount to Bolivia, the Bolivian banks charge both a flat fee and an additional fee per dollar accepted into an account. This often amounts to hundreds of dollars in fees in addition to the fees charged every time funds are deposited to or withdrawn from an account. To minimize the number of transfers, deposits, and withdrawals, we chose to transfer amounts between $25,000 and $50,000 and to time withdrawals in Bolivia to coincide with payment of large expenses such as salaries and bulk purchase of construction materials.

Finally, during the joint meetings we also designed thorough accounting reports for use within the United States. Mano a Mano continued to use these specially designed reports dating from 1999 until 2006, when the IRS changed its requirements for nonprofits working internationally.

*Reporting requirements.* In addition to financial reports, Mano a Mano provides reports on its program activities and accomplishments. The Bolivian-U.S. team also designed reports to track medical distribution, clinic construction, staffing, volunteers, and human resource development. Mano a Mano Bolivia continues to produce these reports on a quarterly basis. They include:

**Medical Distribution**

Number and sources of requests filled for supplies and equipment

**Patient Contacts**

Reason for the patient visit, service/treatment received, number of live births compared to number of deliveries, diagnosis recorded by age and sex of patient, overnight stays, and contacts with community groups

## Clinic Construction

Location of clinics opened, length of time open, size of community, distance from Cochabamba in kilometers and in hours, location and distance of clinics under construction, list of communities with whom an agreement has been signed, and list of applicant communities

## Staffing

Numbers of physicians, nurses, and dentists in each clinic and source of funding for each salary

## Volunteers

Number of volunteers and hours contributed

## Human Resource Development

Number of health-promoter classes and participants, number of continuing education classes and participants

The U.S. office uses these quarterly reports to help monitor progress, manage the organization, prepare grants and related requests for funds, and communicate our activities to donors and volunteers.

*Hiring of staff.* Mano a Mano continued to operate with no paid staff in the United States until 2004. In accordance with the project budget we presented to our anonymous donor, Mano a Mano Bolivia hired additional staff in January 2001. Three part-time positions were made full time: director, accountant, and office assistant. Three new positions were also added: equipment repair and distribution worker, physician, and driver. Most of the new employees hired were known to and trusted by an existing member of Mano a Mano Bolivia. They were also known to have the skills required for these positions and an intense dedication to creating an exceptional organization. More staff members were hired in years two and three of the project.

*Purchase of equipment and vehicles.* Mano a Mano recognized that, as we expanded into more rural Bolivian communities, we needed more equipment and vehicles for: construction, transporting clinic staff, and expanding continuing education of medical personnel and training of volunteer health promoters. The group planned to purchase the large-ticket construction items (e.g., a dump truck, front-end loader, and forklift) on a phased-in schedule based on the numbers of clinics brought into operation over the five-year clinic construction period. We also planned to invest in smaller-scale but equally vital equipment to be used by clinic staff and for continuing education efforts (e.g., motorcycles, TVs, VCRs, two-way radios, overhead projectors, and computers).

## Embarking on the Thirty-Clinic Project

Mano a Mano Bolivia's newly hired staff crowded into its existing office and began to plan the construction of the first year's six clinics and the development of their health-care programs. They carefully calculated the numbers of bricks, beams, tiles, and other items needed, and purchased them in bulk.

When construction was limited to one to two clinics a year, one master carpenter had been able to manage the workload. But six clinics in a year required a different plan. Mano a Mano

Bolivia decided to contract with teams of master builders to decrease the amount of time spent on each clinic and to expand our labor pool. We caucused with the master carpenter who had constructed all previous clinics and trained others to work with him. Those trainees in turn led other teams. Deferring to the master carpenter's expertise, Mano a Mano Bolivia included him in all steps of the process and as a result, we were able to identify concrete and achievable objectives. With the help of the master carpenter and his team, by the end of 2001 three trained teams were building Mano a Mano clinics.

Mano a Mano Bolivia employed a driver to transport the master builder teams to their rural sites. There were sound reasons for incurring this additional expense. Bolivian roads are among the most dangerous in the world, and most Bolivians don't own cars or know how to drive. In addition to transporting builders and construction materials to clinic communities, the driver assumed responsibility for distributing medical supplies.

Mano a Mano continued to utilize the model that had been so successful in building the earlier clinics. The only fundamental change was in the salary payment structure. Beginning with the thirty-clinic project, conversations with a requesting community and its municipal officials always addressed one new requirement—that a governmental entity or other organization must pay the salary of one clinic staff member from opening day and the second salary within three years. When creating programs in its early clinics, Mano a Mano Bolivia had developed excellent relationships with the regional offices of the Ministry of Health. These relationships proved invaluable when seeking commitments for staff salaries. By June 2001, the ministry had agreed to fund two physicians and four nurses in new Mano a Mano clinics, and the recipient municipality had agreed to fund one nurse.

## Accelerating the Thirty-Clinic Project

Six clinics per year were planned and budgeted from 2001 through 2005, but Mano a Mano Bolivia consistently came in under budget. That meant we could capitalize on surplus materials and excess funds and accelerate the pace of progress by building eight clinics during 2001 and ten in 2002. By then, more than seventy communities had made formal requests to partner with Mano a Mano on a clinic project. Given the number of requests and the capacity of Mano a Mano Bolivia to increase the number of clinics brought into operation each year, Segundo and I asked the anonymous donor to accelerate the availability of committed funding. In late 2002, our donor agreed to distribute all grant funds committed to the thirty-clinic project by December 2004.

Based on these accelerated grant payments, Mano a Mano Bolivia was able to accelerate the hiring of staff, the purchase of construction materials and vehicles, and the distribution of medical supplies. Mano a Mano began to build twelve clinics each year. Alongside this accelerated building program, Mano a Mano created consistent health-care services in each clinic and prepared community leaders and municipal officials to co-administer the clinics' operations.

With such rapid growth, the need for offices, storage, and workspaces also grew exponentially. The Cochabamba office soon had twelve staff members and 200,000 pounds of medical supplies and equipment arriving each year from Minnesota. So in 2004 Mano a Mano Bolivia constructed a large office and warehouse building sufficient to accommodate its office staff and the medical distribution program. Later it purchased a lot on which to park its vehicles and heavy equipment. With this supplemental construction project, Mano a Mano Bolivia was able to reduce dramatically its dependence on space the Velásquez family had been providing to support its operation.

The new building made it possible to store boxes of medical

supplies according to category. All wound-care supplies were stored in one section; all substantial medical equipment in another; all drapes and furnishings in another. The new building had ample space for the increasing numbers of Bolivian volunteers who sorted supplies into packages to fill requests from the clinics and other health-care facilities. Over time, Mano a Mano Bolivia also began to manufacture the windows and doors for each construction project, finding in-house manufacture to be more cost effective and of better quality than purchases from other vendors.

## Lessons Learned through the Thirty-Clinic Project

*Develop the model through small-scale, on-the-ground experience before attempting broadscale implementation.* Constructing seven clinics over a period of five years and then creating and managing these clinics' health-care programs gave Mano a Mano the opportunity to examine and improve the community-based model before the expansion phase. For example, the experience with the Gloria clinics led to the decision that all future clinics would belong to the communities in which they were built, not to an organization. The temporary closing of the Campo Vía clinic until the municipality followed through on its agreement to pay the nurse's salary demonstrated the extent to which community residents would stand up for their right to have a government that keeps its word. Communities and municipalities requesting clinics knew of this temporary closing and understood, without having to test it themselves, that Mano a Mano would not work with any group that did not meet its obligations.

*Comprehensive, cross-national planning is critical to success.* Before ramping up the rate of clinic construction, Mano a Mano U.S. and Mano a Mano Bolivia worked together closely to address all of the complicated details regarding banking and accounting, reporting, human resources, equipment, partner roles, construction, and clinic operation.

*Develop solid relationships with Ministry of Health personnel.* The Bolivian Ministry of Health considers each Mano a Mano clinic to be the official health-care provider in the designated geographical area. The ministry sets goals for all facilities and requires detailed monthly reports on patients seen. The ministry and Mano a Mano personnel had worked together for five years before expansion funding became available. The mutual understanding, confidence, and trust that Mano a Mano Bolivia had nurtured throughout this initial relationship enabled the organization to negotiate successfully with the ministry for payment of clinic staff salaries.

*Integrate long-term sustainability into the model.* Long-term sustainability was always a primary consideration in planning the clinic program expansion. The question was whether, if Mano a Mano U.S. ceased to operate, the clinics could continue in operation without Mano a Mano's payment of staff salaries, and if so, how. One means of addressing this question was to require a governmental entity or other organization to pay for one clinic staff salary from opening day and the second salary within three years. Adhering to these criteria has enabled the clinics to become self-sufficient. By the end of 2001, Mano a Mano could see that its premise was sound and viable.

*Create training materials for clinic construction.* Mano a Mano Bolivia trained and mobilized additional teams of master builders as needed to meet construction timelines without sacrificing quality. The training materials standardized building specifications across teams.

## Communities Request Help to Build
## Sanitation and Education Infrastructure

As rural residents experienced success in their clinic-related partnerships, they began to ask Mano a Mano to work with them on other projects. Through the health education offered by their clinics, residents of these communities learned that a lack of clean drinking water and absence of sanitation facilities presented serious health hazards. Springs, streams, and rivers in rural areas often carry human and animal waste, laundry soap, and trash. Clinic staff members and villagers came to understand that these springs, streams, and rivers, which function as the village's primary water source, must be protected.

To this end, health education offered by the clinic staff taught residents to: boil drinking water, dispose of human waste in a way that would not pollute rivers and streams, and separate drinking water from that which had been used for bathing or laundry. Encouraging villagers to abide by these simple principles has significantly reduced infectious diseases. Combining health education with basic sanitation enables a community to better manage health risks over the long term. Building sanitation facilities was a natural complement to the clinic projects.

In response to requests for help improving sanitation, Mano a Mano applied for and received grants to launch sanitation projects. These grants fund the construction of brick buildings that include separate bathrooms for boys and girls, each with individual toilet stalls, sinks, and showers. The facilities are built next to the community school to support formal hygiene instruction classes and students' daily hygiene practices.

Water is pumped to a tank that sits on the sanitation building's roof and is heated by solar panels. When Mano a Mano's first sanitation project opened, excited students lined up for their first opportunity to turn on the sink faucet and feel warm water. A modern septic system similar to those used for the Mano a Mano clinics holds waste from the facility. To encourage residents to stop washing their clothing in local streams and rivers, Mano a Mano built laundry tubs with exterior water faucets. School personnel, clinic staff, and health promoters teach children and adults the importance of using these facilities.

Partnering with Mano a Mano on the construction contributed to communities' almost tangible feeling of empowerment. Through the knowledge that they were capable of completing complex projects and responsibly managing them, villagers gained confidence and determination. Knowing that they were able to co-administer a health-care clinic and operate modern sanitation facilities, residents turned their attention to other urgent unmet needs. Most targeted improving educational facilities and youth opportunities.

This was true in Campo Vibora where a young father lamented, "We are responsible to give teachers a place to live, but we can barely afford houses for our own families. Our teachers have been living in little sheds that should be for animals but we just didn't have any other place for them." Emboldened by the knowledge that they could successfully petition to construct and maintain health-care facilities, the father and his neighbors turned to Mano a Mano to meet another urgent community need. Community leaders presented Mano a Mano with plans that detailed what they could contribute to future projects, including schools and living quarters for their teachers. They petitioned government officials to pay teachers to work and live in their villages. These initiatives reflect the democratic process at its most basic grassroots level.

Villagers have been, and continue to be, the driving force behind a dramatic transformation in rural Bolivian education. Until recently, schools in most rural areas have typically consisted of dilapidated buildings, one-room adobe structures without doors or windows, or simply benches under trees. Now there are brick-and-mortar buildings that include comfortable living quarters for teachers. Instead of fleeing back to metropolitan areas after a few days or weeks on the job, teachers now stay at their posts. In Campo Vibora that has meant one young father can set aside his shame and envision a life for his children that is not inevitably a future of extreme material poverty. "Now we have eight teachers. They stay in our community and teach our children."

Mano a Mano took seriously every community request to partner on an education infrastructure project, but we wanted to ensure that taking on new projects did not jeopardize the growing clinic program. The board expanded the organization's mission and decided to build sanitation, classroom, and teacher housing projects if and when funds became available.

Successful fundraising efforts made it possible to undertake these projects using Mano a Mano's standard partnership approach. Once all parties agreed on their contributions, they signed an agreement and scheduled the work. School and teacher housing projects differ in one significant respect from the clinic model. Mano a Mano does not administer schools. Education infrastructure, once completed, belongs to the community and its municipal government. All agreements for these projects include a clause that requires these buildings be used for their intended purpose unless Mano a Mano agrees to an alternate use.

## EXPANDED MISSION STATEMENT, DECEMBER 2004

Mission: To improve the health and extend the life span of impoverished Bolivians by increasing the capacity of health-care providers and communities to address their medical, community-development, and educational needs.

## Improving Roads and Airstrips

The budget that Mano a Mano presented to our anonymous donor included line items for heavy equipment. Given the difficulty of reaching many rural communities, particularly with truckloads of building supplies, Mano a Mano Bolivia realized it needed to improve entrance roads to its clinic communities. We also began to improve aircraft landing strips located near clinic communities. Each of these projects was done in response to a community request and followed the same community involvement model.

### A 2004 VISIT TO A LOWLAND VILLAGE

When Segundo and I finished interviewing the clinic medical staff, about a hundred villagers eagerly waited to show us the school and teacher housing that Mano a Mano had also helped them build.

The teachers were ecstatic with their quarters. They had taken great effort to beautify their units with pictures. "We will stay here. We're not going anywhere else," the teachers beamed.

One described the shack he lived in when he first came to the community. "When I cooked my soup (eaten every day), the smoke from the fire would make the bugs in the thatched roof drunk and they'd fall into my soup. I'm so happy to be living in this clean place, where I can eat a bowl of soup without bugs falling into it."

After showing us their brick school, they took us to see the three-sided wood structure with a thatched roof that had served as a classroom before the school. It was about thirty feet by fifteen feet with a dirt floor and no windows. It was dark, despite the tiny slivers of light shining in through the cracks between the wood planks in the wall. One of the villagers said, "Now that we have beautiful classrooms, many more children are coming to school. So many, that we have to use the old classroom again. Will Mano a Mano help us build more classrooms?"

## Lessons Learned in Building Sanitation and Education Infrastructure

*Helping communities address a problem empowers them to solve other unmet needs.* Once communities have partnered to build a clinic and co-manage its operation, they gain a sense of power to pursue other improvements and address other unmet needs with the government, Mano a Mano, and other organizations.

*Apply the basic Mano a Mano model beyond building clinics.* The basic model is one in which the community owns and is central to the project, the municipal government contributes, and all project participants enter into a written agreement defining roles and responsibilities. The basic model envisions a project implemented in Bolivia by Bolivians with Mano a Mano U.S. board oversight.

*Require that the building be used as intended over the long term.* Mano a Mano includes a clause in its agreements with the community and municipality that a building constructed by Mano a Mano can only be used for its intended purpose unless we accept a proposed change in its use. This clause protects community residents from anyone who might decide to expropriate the building for personal use in the future.

◆ ◆ ◆ ◆

In Phase III, Mano a Mano successfully ramped up from building one or two clinics per year to building eight to twelve clinics per year in addition to new sanitation and education infrastructure. An ever-growing number of rural Bolivians gained access to higher-quality health care and became empowered to address other urgent unmet needs. This successful acceleration of the community clinic program was built on the solid foundation of detailed planning undertaken by Mano a Mano U.S. and Mano a Mano Bolivia's leadership team.

# 6

# Aviation Program Created to Support Expanded Service Area

*Aviation is proof that given the will, we have the capacity to achieve the impossible.*
**Attributed to Eddie Rickenbacker, American aviator**

Stunning landscapes often thwart the best intentions. That's certainly the case in Bolivia, where mountainous terrain impedes humanitarian efforts to extend the benefits of improved health care and education to remote areas, and poor road systems often frustrate rescue efforts. As requests to partner with Mano a Mano spanned a wider and wider geographic area, transportation became increasingly difficult. Beginning in 2002 (during Phase III), Mano a Mano took to the skies to help overcome the ground transportation barriers to many communities in remote Bolivia.

Bolivia's road infrastructure consists primarily of two-lane gravel roads that connect the country's principal cities to each other, plus minimal arterial roads that lead to those main roads. Roads through the high Andes, where most Mano a Mano projects are located, wind their way along steep mountainsides that slow traffic to less than twenty miles per hour. Many rural communities don't have access to even the most basic arterial roads. Mano a Mano Bolivia purchased vehicles as its service area expanded and used them to visit rural communities throughout all project phases. Where needed, Mano a Mano's heavy equipment was used to clear a roadway into a community so trucks could deliver construction materials.

Because requests began to arrive from communities located as far as 475 miles from Cochabamba, the Mano a Mano U.S. board began to consider flights in small aircraft as a transportation alternative. Segundo was aware of a Lutheran mission in Cochabamba that owned a Cessna 206 six-passenger aircraft that it used to transport missionaries into similar areas. He approached a Wisconsin foundation with a strong interest in aviation and requested funds to purchase flight hours for Mano a Mano from the Lutheran mission.

The foundation granted sufficient funding to cover eighty hours of flight time. Mano a Mano Bolivia used these flight hours for three purposes—first, to reduce the extensive travel time required for staff to reach the increasingly remote communities. Use of the aircraft often reduced a twenty-hour mountain drive to a two-hour flight. Without this air option, Mano a Mano simply could not have extended its reach into many of these remote communities. The air time was also used to transport critically ill and injured patients whose medical emergencies could not be managed in a community clinic, and to fly volunteer medical professionals into tropical areas on weekends to serve tribal populations.

The Mano a Mano U.S. office maintained close contact with the granting foundation through quarterly flight reports and frequent phone conversations that recounted the details of specific flights. The aviation donor was especially touched by the stories of lives saved through emergency flights, including the following account from a Mano a Mano clinic in San Agustín, which is a seventeen-hour drive from Cochabamba:

> *Family members of a patient with severe abdominal pain had rushed him to the community clinic on a donkey, their only means of transportation. Recognizing that this patient's appendix had nearly burst during the long and strenuous journey, the clinic physician immediately radioed for the aircraft and began administering medication. The aircraft arrived within three hours and transported the patient with his family to a hospital in the city of Potosí. Following an appendectomy and treatment to prevent infection, the patient returned home, grateful that the airlift program had saved his life.*

## Creation of a Second Bolivian NGO to Manage Aviation

When the Lutheran mission that owned the aircraft decided to sell its aviation program in 2004, the Wisconsin-based foundation who had paid for flight hours granted funds to Mano a Mano to make a transformative purchase. It included the Cessna 206 aircraft, a hangar at the Cochabamba airport, tools for maintenance, and some spare aircraft parts. Mano a Mano created a second Bolivian counterpart organization, Mano a Mano Apoyo Aéreo (MMAA), to own and manage the aviation program.

The directors of the foundation required that the aviation program be incorporated as a Bolivian nonprofit separate from Mano a Mano Bolivia. They stipulated that MMAA's board of directors must include members with aviation expertise to direct the program. The foundation also indicated that the aviation program must be run with the intent to generate funds. The donor foundation's directors were familiar with other aviation programs that underutilized their aircraft and pilots. They expected MMAA to be cost conscious and draw Bolivian revenue into the program, aiming to ultimately become self-financing. The creation of a separate entity also protected Mano a Mano Bolivia's extensive resources (office and warehouse, heavy machinery, vehicles, and funds) in the case of a liability claim.

Mano a Mano follows our donors' wishes when accepting funds and allocates them solely to the donor-identified project. In this case, the Mano a Mano U.S. board agreed that these donor requirements were reasonable and in the best interests of the entire Mano a Mano network. We accepted the donation of the aviation program, requirements and all, and proceeded to create our new aviation organization.

Prior to the creation of MMAA, Mano a Mano Bolivia had worked in collaboration with Mano a Mano U.S. to establish the process for use of flight hours. The Mano a Mano Bolivia director had also expressed a strong interest in managing the aviation program and had opposed the incorporation of another organization to perform that role. This difference of opinion marked the first significant disagreement within Mano a Mano. It resulted in extensive discussion and finally a decision to move forward.

Once a board of directors for the aviation organization was established, the Mano a Mano U.S. board worked closely with the new MMAA board to agree on four goals: provide safe, efficient, and reliable air transport to support Mano a Mano's programs in rural Bolivia; increase aviation capacity in Bolivia by training pilots and technicians; create and operate an emergency-response program; and generate income to help cover operating costs.

MMAA developed or expanded the following programs to support Mano a Mano programs in rural Bolivia:

## Weekend Clinics

Tribe members suffering from the ravages of parasites, those debilitated by pain after extracting their own abscessed teeth, incessantly coughing children, and others came to rely on a weekend clinic program that Mano a Mano Bolivia established with a portion of its flight hours. The patients in question live in Bolivia's tropical Beni department (state). It is nearly impossible to reach them in a timely fashion by any means other than flight.

Transportation into these regions presents a daunting challenge. Bolivia's two main cities are connected by a narrow two-lane road, but there are no roads to outlying areas. Rivers connect some settlements, but their width (several times that of the Mississippi), rapid currents, and large amounts of debris are dangerous for even the most experienced boaters. Small aircraft transport continues to provide the only feasible means for reaching these isolated communities.

Mano a Mano Bolivia recognized the need for health care in these remote areas and responded by offering its professional volunteers the opportunity to staff weekend clinics. Several Cochabamba physicians, nurses, pharmacists, and dentists began contributing weekends to this cause. Working with MMAA and the ranchers who come into contact with the tribal groups, two weekend trips each month are scheduled. The weekend clinic concept builds on Mano a Mano's dual experience with developing and managing a successful aviation program and creating and co-administering its network of community clinics.

The Beni has grass airstrips on which small aircraft can land safely. Ten villages have built airstrips near land on which tribal groups live and hunt. Shortly before a scheduled weekend clinic, nuns from the Catholic mission closest to the airstrip typically coordinate with tribal leaders to inform their groups that a clinic will be held on a specific day. Word of the clinic travels quickly through the area and dozens of people appear at dawn on the scheduled day. As soon as the aircraft touches down on the grass landing strip, the volunteers set up the clinic.

If a building is available, volunteers create room dividers

with sheets and wire. If there is no building, they string wire or cording between trees and hang sheets. Volunteers organize themselves according to specialty and then divide the waiting patients into groups. Benita Diaz, a pediatric nurse who participates in weekend clinics, said, "We literally run from one patient to the next because so many people want to see us. Knowing that people feel much better because I have been here to treat them motivates me to continue doing this volunteer work."

No person can be idle regardless of their training. Even the pilots assist by recording the limited available patient medical history, managing the crowd, or entertaining the many children who accompany their parents. Throughout the day, physicians and nurses diagnose and treat dozens of patients whose complaints may include machete wounds, animal bites, parasites, diarrhea, and respiratory infections. Many weekend clinics include dentists to provide dental care and oral hygiene education. If the volunteers determine that immediate hospital care is indicated, the patient, together with family members, is flown to an appropriate hospital.

## Emergency Rescue

After assuming responsibility for the aviation program, MMAA expanded into emergency rescue to respond to calls from outside the Mano a Mano clinic network. The majority of these calls come from tropical areas and generally from ranchers or nuns with short-wave radios. One pilot describes a rescue flight:

> In Ushbe, a small community typical of those located in Bolivia's Amazon region, a major windstorm felled a huge tree onto a family of five's small house. Constructed of cane, the house could not sustain the weight of the tree and was completely destroyed. Unfortunately the whole family was at home, protecting themselves from the cold wind. On most days they would have been hunting for their food.

*All five of them suffered serious wounds. Ushbe has neither a health clinic nor medical personnel. Its residents called Mano a Mano via short-wave radio, confident that we would air-rescue the family and fly them to health care in Cochabamba. Mano a Mano responded and took family members to the hospital within a few hours of receiving word. The time involved in this response and air rescue by MMAA stands in contrast to what would have entailed a trip of at least five days by any other form of transportation.*

*Once the family arrived in Cochabamba, an ambulance from the SAR (Save and Rescue) volunteer group took them to the city hospital. Emergency room physicians found that each family member had multiple fractures and sent them immediately to surgery. Sadly, one of the children died. The physicians told us that emergency surgery saved the lives of the other two children, who almost certainly would have died as well within a few hours.*

A few days after the Ushbe rescue flight, the same pilot received an urgent request to respond to an accident in which a busload of students near Potosí had veered off a mountain road and rolled over several times. Many passengers were seriously injured. The pilot quickly removed the seats from the aircraft and hung hammocks to create a two-tier passenger compartment. After landing on the road, he flew four injured students to a city hospital. All survived.

Given space limitations, MMAA pilots typically fly alone when responding to an emergency request. Accidents often involve more than one patient. In other circumstances, family members may be needed to assist with care. Pilots often must convince family members to choose which of them should accompany the patient and which belongings must be left at home. MMAA pilots have attended first responder training sessions with medical personnel from Minnesota to learn to apply first aid and stabilize patients before placing them in the aircraft. Pilots must also calm the family and place everyone in the safest possible position in the aircraft before returning to the city. The limited capacity of a six-passenger aircraft forces pilots to consider the weight and need for every item transported. Weight also limits the amount of rescue equipment that can be included on the flight.

## Emergency Food and Supply Airlift

Flooding in Bolivia's tropical regions isolated tribal families from much of their food supply during the heavy tropical rains of 2009 and 2010. To assist with natural disasters such as this, MMAA flew twenty-pound packages of basic food supplies to airstrips in the area, where local nuns helped distribute the food. Mano a Mano paid for the food and MMAA staff purchased and packaged it. This program continues to serve disaster areas when the need arises.

## Income-Generating Efforts

To meet its goal of generating income in Bolivia to support the aviation program, MMAA transports cargo, flies private individuals, and performs maintenance on aircraft owned by businesses and private individuals.

MMAA transports cargo for other organizations, businesses, or individuals on one leg of its Mano a Mano-related flights. The usual load consists of personal items, but MMAA has on occasion cleared space to fly small livestock by storing seats in the back portion of the aircraft. After each such flight, the technicians thoroughly clean and disinfect the aircraft.

MMAA sometimes flies paying passengers to their chosen destinations within Bolivia. Examples include insurance companies whose patients require specialized care that cannot be provided at their current location and tourists who wish to visit areas that are not served by the Bolivian airlines. Another example is a businessman who makes routine trips between Cochabamba and Oruro and does not wish to drive this time-consuming route.

The Bolivian government's aviation authority (DGAC) enforces essentially the same requirements as the U.S. Federal Aviation Authority to ensure safety. These rules require strict adherence to a maintenance schedule. MMAA operates the only aviation facility in Cochabamba that holds the licenses required to complete major maintenance as well as routine service on single- and twin-engine aircraft. It charges owners of private aircraft to perform these services.

## Challenges of Mano a Mano Apoyo Aéreo

The aviation program initially included one aircraft, a hangar adjacent to the Cochabamba airport, some spare parts, and two volunteer pilots. These were all truly valuable gifts. However, operating funds were not included. We intended that MMAA earn sufficient revenue in Bolivia to cover basic operating costs. Mano a Mano U.S. worked with MMAA to define all costs, calculate an amount to charge for flight hours, and determine billing rates for different customer types.

MMAA bills other Mano a Mano programs at the actual cost of operation, including charges for staff, fuel, maintenance, replacement parts, and insurance. Each Mano a Mano program includes a line item in its budget to cover needed air transport. Similarly, when any of the other nonprofits that operate in Bolivia request an MMAA flight, they are also billed at the actual cost of operation. Private persons or businesses are charged the generally accepted market rate, which covers operational costs, a reserve amount for future engine and propeller replacement, and profit.

MMAA projects its budget based on anticipated fees from these groups and responsibly balances the number of flights it makes in each category in order to cover its expenses. MMAA attempts to reserve approximately half of the available flight hours for Mano a Mano's program needs such as staff travel, weekend clinics, and emergency airlift. Approximately one-quarter of MMAA's hours are offered to organizations with similar missions. During the remaining quarter of the total flight hours, the aircraft are used to generate income by providing flights to individuals and businesses. When MMAA can maintain this balanced mix, the program is self-funding.

MMAA must operate within extensive rules and regulations. Several Bolivian agencies control air transport, and maintaining constructive relationships with each is imperative. MMAA complies with all regulatory requirements—and then goes beyond timely compliance to network with agency personnel and assure their familiarity with MMAA programs and operations. As is the case with all Mano a Mano programs, there is never any attempt to bribe officials to expedite work. MMAA recognizes that each air control agency has a distinct purpose and different responsibilities.

The Dirección General de Aeronáutica Civil (DGAC) controls aviation in much the same way that the Federal Aviation Administration (FAA) does in the United States. All aircraft inspections and maintenance must be recorded according to DGAC specifications and those of the manufacturer. The Administración de Aeropuertos y Servicios Auxiliares a la Navegación Aérea (AASANA) requires that a flight plan be filed each time an aircraft leaves the airport. All MMAA flights, including emergencies, begin with a filed flight plan.

The Bolivian Air Force must approve certain flights. In its attempt to gain control over drug trafficking, the Bolivian government has designated many of its tropical areas as "red zones," and approval is required for all flights into those areas. This presents a significant challenge for MMAA because eighty percent of its emergency flights are requested from a red zone. One late Friday afternoon MMAA received an urgent call to rescue a young woman from the Beni region who had been in labor but unable to deliver for nearly four days. MMAA's pilot Captain Martinez worried that he might not get permission to fly into a red zone, but knew that this patient and her infant would die unless he could get them to a hospital. The only air force general who could approve the request had left for the weekend. After dozens of persistent phone calls, Martinez located the general and received permission to fly the next morning. He contacted the nun who had telephoned and asked her to prepare the woman for the flight. In the morning, her family brought her to the edge of the runway and flew with her to Cochabamba where she received a Caesarian section. The following week she returned home with a healthy baby, whom she named for the pilot.

The Dirección General de Substancias Controladas (DGSC) controls the number of aircraft and amount of diesel fuel that can be purchased in Bolivia at one time due to concerns that it will be diverted to illegal drug-related activities. At the time of purchase, fuel must be loaded directly into the aircraft or the fuel tank at the MMAA hangar. It cannot legally be carried in or loaded into any other type of container. Each month MMAA must file a report with the DGSC indicating hours flown and fuel used. Given this level of control over fuel, others have approached MMAA personnel with requests. For example, an individual approached them recently with a request to purchase fuel from their tank. He offered to pay the organization any amount they asked, a tempting offer for anyone with a tight budget. Staff members immediately recognized the illegal nature of the request, declined it, and informed the MMAA board. Personnel in Bolivia often face this type of enticement.

The U.S. Drug Enforcement Administration (DEA) had a major presence in Bolivia for several years. Because small aircraft have been used extensively to transport illegal substances in South America, the DEA carefully monitored aviation. Each time an aircraft took off or landed in Cochabamba, dogs sniffed inside the cabin and all exterior surfaces of the plane before it moved out of or into the hangar.

Planes and personnel both require scrutiny. MMAA takes great care in making background checks prior to hiring personnel in order to avoid any interaction with drug traffickers. Shortly after the organization was founded, the MMAA board found itself in the midst of a serious internal dispute when board members began hearing about a newly hired pilot, his background, and an incident that had occurred twenty years earlier. The pilot had been arrested, but never tried, for transporting illegal substances. Although he had been released and not convicted of any crime, some board members did not trust him. Others took the position that he should be considered innocent until a court found him guilty. After several days of intense discussion, the board broke off its discussion without resolution when the pilot himself decided he did not wish to work in an environment of suspicion and left the organization. The experience did not change MMAA's hiring practices except to strengthen the resolve to carefully check the background of any potential hire with particular attention to the possibility of involvement in the drug trade.

Aircraft maintenance is subject to stringent rules based on the type of plane and the frequency of its use. Lengthy delays in obtaining new parts can result in extended down time when the aircraft can neither serve program needs nor produce revenue. MMAA tries to avoid maintenance down time by maintaining an inventory of frequently needed items, such as a starter, magnetos, hoses, and rivets of various types and sizes. MMAA also anticipates needs for replacement parts based on hours flown and informs the U.S. office when it will require a replacement that is not available in Bolivia. The U.S. office purchases and transports those parts. Travelers may take small parts in their luggage. Mano a Mano may send larger parts in a shipping container with medical cargo. In spite of these preventative efforts, the limited capacity to support aviation in Bolivia presents continual challenges.

While Bolivia has an abundant supply of trained medical and education professionals, it suffers from a serious shortage of trained pilots and aircraft technicians. When MMAA incorporated, it had the good fortune of being directed by a Swedish pilot who had flown small aircraft throughout Bolivia for over thirty years. His leadership made it possible for MMAA to establish itself as a nonprofit in Bolivia. When he retired, MMAA hired a highly qualified pilot who had flown for another nonprofit in Bolivia for several years. Over time, MMAA has developed a reputation as a well-run, safe, and strictly legal operation. With concerted effort on the part of board members in both Bolivia and the United States, MMAA now has two full-time pilots and another two who fly on an as-needed basis, plus two full-time technicians.

Just as commercial airlines must allow pilots to rest for a specified number of hours between flights, small aviation programs must do the same. MMAA maintains a roster of backup pilots for this reason.

For MMAA, scheduling is more complicated than just ensuring pilot rest. Nearly seventy percent of the organization's flights are destined for a red zone. The majority of emergency calls come from the tropics and almost all weekend clinics serve tribal groups who live there. Since flights to a red zone must be approved by the Bolivian Air Force, whose office personnel aren't available on weekends, MMAA flights must be planned in advance. In collaboration with Mano a Mano Bolivia, MMAA schedules weekend clinics for the entire year each January and requests approval of the schedule. However, getting approval for emergency flights becomes more challenging when emergencies occur on weekends. Pilots often spend precious time attempting to reach officials in order to obtain the required permission for an MMAA weekend flight into a tribal area. Fortunately in the following emergency, the pilot reached an officer who released the flight. Later the pilot recounted:

> *On Sunday morning, the MMAA office received an urgent radio call from the jungle village of Oromomo. Viviana, a six-year-old Yuracaré girl, had been pushed into an open fire by another child. She was severely burned over sixty percent of her body—the back part of her head, all of her back to below her bottom, down her left leg to above the foot, above the knee of her right leg, most of her right arm to the shoulder, and her right hand. Most of the burns were third degree.*
>
> *When the aircraft arrived, I used a sheet to carry Viviana to the airplane and to hold her hammock-style during the flight. Two Yuracaré women traveled to Cochabamba with her. We learned from them that Viviana's mother had died three years earlier and that she had no other family. She had wandered from one home to another and was finally taken in by a family to assist with their work.*
>
> *Viviana was placed in the burn unit of Cochabamba's public hospital. She received multiple blood transfusions, proteins, and antibiotics to fight infection. Over the next two months, Viviana had surgery about every ten days. Her pain was so great that she cried and couldn't eat for three days after each one. But her care was excellent and her spirit strong. Now Viviana runs all over the place, climbs, jumps, and plays tag. She lives in an orphanage and is a very happy child.*

Initiating the aviation program presented Mano a Mano with a new challenge. Many of its communities had no field on which aircraft could land. One of the construction equipment operators described their deliberations about how to construct a landing strip near the clinic village of Chunca Cancha:

> *The village council asked us to build a runway in the only flat area near the town, but we thought it would be impossible. Yet the people were very persistent and we knew they would*

*work well with us, since we had had very good experience with other projects in this community. We told them, "The mountains are very high and the land is narrow. We don't see how a runway can be built here."*

*But we studied the topography and the wind currents and finally came up with an idea that we thought would work. It would mean that we would have to chop off the peak of the mountain and fill in a ravine. Removing the mountain peak would allow for a safe approach and filling the ravine would allow for a sufficiently long airstrip. With measurements and a plan in hand, we consulted with our pilot and flew over the site for a final look so he could decide. He said, "Yes, go ahead. This will work."*

*So we built the airstrip with a "crew cut" to the mountain, moving hundreds and hundreds of truckloads of fill with excellent participation from the community.*

*The day after we finished and had begun to haul the equipment back to Cochabamba, the office received a call from the doctor in the Chunca Cancha clinic saying they had a patient who would die in childbirth unless a Caesarian section could be performed. The aircraft transported her to the hospital in Cochabamba. When we heard that this mom and her baby had returned home in good health, we knew God had led us to make the right decision.*

Even when a community has an airstrip, challenges remain. Grass or gravel landing areas must be maintained properly in order for aircraft to land safely. Animals or debris on the runway, softening of the airstrip surface by heavy rains, and wind and water erosion can create serious problems.

Before an aircraft flies into an area requiring landing on a rural strip, as contrasted with an airport runway, the pilot contacts a designated person in the area via short-wave radio. That individual, selected by the community, assumes responsibility for assessing whether the strip is safe. MMAA has an airstrip assessment training program for these individuals and provides tools with which to measure ground density. MMAA is able to use the twenty-one airstrips constructed by its counterpart NGOs.

## Lessons Learned in the Aviation Program

*Recruit specialized experts in the aviation field to manage the program.* Operating an aviation program presents a unique set of challenges in addition to those encountered with other service programs and should not be attempted without this expertise.

*Train all personnel to follow stringent requirements and keep complete records.* An aviation program simply cannot succeed if it does not follow the regulations and document its adherence to all aviation requirements. Safety is the top priority.

*Seek personnel who are committed to service.* All MMAA staff complete tasks that would not be included in most aviation job descriptions.

*Anticipate and guard against enticements to engage in illegal activity.* At the outset, MMAA board members made an unequivocal decision that the organization would not attempt to bribe a public official under any circumstances. The temptation and pressure to make a payment or sell something illegally is constant and powerful. We felt that, as an organization, we needed to be clear with everyone that Mano a Mano would not become involved in this type of activity. For Mano a Mano, adherence to this principle remains paramount.

*Carefully calculate costs.* Simply put, safe flight requires adequate financing. We have learned that a make-do attitude functions with other programs as long as persons are willing to live on less and work long hours. Not so with aviation. Costly plane parts, such as a new engine, must be replaced or over-hauled at a specified number of hours. The organization cannot postpone that sort of purchase and decide to fly anyway. Each annual budget must reflect these costs and identify sources of revenue to cover them.

Mano a Mano took advantage of the great aerial highway to overcome ground transportation barriers to fulfilling its mission. This enabled the organization to provide safe, efficient, and reliable air transport to support Mano a Mano's programs in rural Bolivia, and to create and operate an emergency response program.

# 7

# Creating Infrastructure for Rural Economic Development

*Water is life. It's the briny broth of our origins, the pounding circulatory system of the world.... We stake our civilizations on the coasts and mighty rivers. Our deepest dread is the threat of having too little—or too much.*
**—Barbara Kingsolver, author and 2011 Dayton Literary Peace Prize winner**[55]

From 2005 on, Mano a Mano has responded to community requests for water and road projects. Echoing Kingsolver's sentiments, a Laguna Sulti community member stated, "We know that Mano a Mano helps with many different kinds of projects but, for us, the most important is water. Water is life. Without water we have nothing."

In December 2004, the U.S. board agreed to amend Mano a Mano's mission statement to explicitly include education infrastructure projects and better position the organization to pursue requested water and road projects. In 2005, the board revised our statement's wording to more clearly reflect this expanded mission.

## BOARD APPROVED MISSION STATEMENT IN 2005

Mission Statement: To create partnerships with impoverished Bolivian communities to improve health and increase economic well-being.

## Creating a New Organization—Mano a Mano Nuevo Mundo

During 2005, Mano a Mano created its third Bolivian counterpart organization, Mano a Mano Nuevo Mundo (Spanish for *New World*) or MMNM, to focus on economic development. Mano a Mano chose to establish another separate entity as a means to pursue new funding opportunities, manage liability, recognize a separate focus from Mano a Mano Bolivia (MMB) and MMAA, and pursue additional project possibilities. The U.S. board initially hoped MMB would transfer its heavy machines to the new organization so all heavy equipment work could be consolidated. Eventually we decided, however, not to request the transfer given concerns that it would reignite tensions that had stemmed from creating the aviation program. The U.S. board concluded it would be best not to tamper with MMB's excellent implementation of its own programs.

While the division of heavy equipment between two organizations has resulted in some duplication of efforts, in general the types of projects undertaken by MMB and MMNM have differed in scope and purpose. The U.S. board seeks financial support for road projects undertaken by MMNM separate and apart from funding requests for MMB's community clinic projects, for which road construction may be undertaken by MMB incidental to the building of clinics and schools.

Once MMNM had a board of directors in place, the Mano a Mano U.S. board worked closely with it to develop goals for the organization. The two boards jointly agreed on four primary goals for MMNM:

- Increase capacity of rural Bolivian communities to raise sufficient quantities and varieties of food to feed their families a healthy diet.

- Expand capacity of farm families to produce crops and livestock for sale.

- Build roads on which these commodities can be transported to markets.

- Reduce soil erosion in order to maintain the viability of agricultural land, recognizing that erosion results from flooding in the rainy season and wind during the dry season.

The goals were addressed through the water reservoir and road building projects undertaken by MMNM.

## Agricultural Water Projects

Having witnessed Mano a Mano's success in creating a network of rural clinics and the infrastructure for education, communities began to approach the organization to assist with their most pressing issue: lack of water. After the creation of MMNM, Mano a Mano redirected requests to that organization.

So far, most community requests for water projects have come from the Cochabamba Valley, which is situated in central Bolivia. Here the farmers generally own one- to two-acre plots on which they raise corn, potatoes, or small grains. The valley essentially has two climatic seasons—a warm, rainy season during which rain falls nearly every day for two or three months, and a cooler dry season when rain is rare. Farmers plant in August, hoping for early rains that, along with melted mountain snow, will trickle into their streams and begin to flow through their earthen canals. In good years, crops germinate and reach the half-mature stage before heavy rains begin in December. If the rainy season brings sufficient water, farmers direct the water to channels and irrigate their fields, watering crops to maturity in March. During years of light snowmelt or limited rainfall, lack of water results in a widespread failure of seeds to germinate along with substantially reduced yields. In contrast, during years of heavy snow or excessive rainfall, fields flood, washing away germinating seeds and sprouting plants. Heavy flooding creates added danger by undermining the foundations of adobe homes, leading to total structural collapse and serious injury or death for occupants.

For centuries, the Incas in Bolivia's high Andean mountains and valleys built structures to retain water in the December-to-February rainy season to release to fields during the dry season. The Incas collected and channeled rainwater through an extensive and intricate canal network. While centuries of war and neglect have destroyed the bulk of these systems, farmers still maintain shallow canals to channel water when it is available.

Building on the Incan tradition, MMNM initiated its first water project to increase the capacity of a modest-sized earthen reservoir in the rural Bolivian village of Ucuchi near Cochabamba. In 2004, during the signing of an agreement between MMB and the Ucuchi community to build classrooms, local men approached the road construction manager with a plea for help in increasing and repairing their water reservoir. They led the manager to side-by-side plots, showing him one that had access to water while the other did not. One yielded a mass of bright red strawberries; the other lay parched and brown. The availability of water made the difference between a viable capacity to produce food and total crop failure. The plea was repeated a few months later. During the dedication of the new Ucuchi public school, Doña Martina approached Mano a Mano with both a problem and a solution:

*Please, señores, we have worked hard together to build the school and now our children can have hope for the future. But we are desperate to solve another problem. We have good land but not enough water to keep crops alive. Our water runs away and the corn produces little, or dies of thirst. We know that a bigger water reservoir would hold enough rainwater to channel to fields as our ancestors did. Please help us again. You know we have ganas (motivation) and will work every day if you bring your machines and build with us. Then we could feed our children and sell the rest in the city.*

A few weeks later, Doña Martina's plea was followed by a formal request from the community of Ucuchi and their municipal officials for Mano a Mano's assistance in expanding the capacity of its water reservoir. This request presented an excellent opportunity to pilot a modest-sized project in a community whose residents had shown considerable capacity to work together for the common good. It involved enlarging an already existing reservoir by raising the levee wall to increase its holding capacity.

The combination of dire need and the potential for funding from Bolivian governmental entities, as well as from the United States, led to the decision to accept the water project request. Mano a Mano applied for and received a grant from a family foundation focused on improving access to water. With funding from this foundation, plus the municipal government and community contributions, MMNM completed the Ucuchi project the following year. According to the municipal agronomist, farmers who received water from the reservoir for the first time saw their productivity and income double. Completing this pilot project on time, within budget, and with a successful outcome led Mano a Mano to add water projects as a means to fulfill the community development portion of its mission.

Soon leaders of other communities began to approach their municipal officials with desperate pleas for water projects, recognizing that Mano a Mano did not consider requests unless there was municipality participation. Over the last decade, many rural Bolivian municipalities had decided to allocate a major part of their annual budgets to water and road projects. Given this trend, Mano a Mano decided to take on more requests for water and road projects. MMNM applied the standard Mano a Mano model including the same key components to each project that it accepted.

The organization's first request to build an entire reservoir came from the community of Laguna Sulti and its municipality. In response, Mano a Mano negotiated a partnership agreement to build a reservoir and then invited the entire community to hear about and vote on the proposal. Hundreds attended the meeting, including many who endured great hardship to travel to the site. Doña Fausta, leaning on her walker for support, trekked more than a mile to be present for the vote because, as she said, "Without water for our fields, we will not live." Residents voted unanimously to approve the agreement.

During the dedication of the Laguna Sulti water reservoir the following year, Don Nicolas, one of the community leaders, said, "We have learned how to work with Mano a Mano and we know that Mano a Mano delivers. The road from Cochabamba to Sucre is sowed with Mano a Mano projects."

Mano a Mano received funds from the St. Paul Rotary Club and Rotary International to complete the Laguna Sulti project. When Rotarians from Minnesota visited the project, residents told them, "Without water we have nothing. Many of our men go to the city to find work because their fields do not produce and they cannot feed their families. Every drop of water is important to us—we do not waste a cupful."

In 2010, MMNM completed its third reservoir and its most challenging project so far in the high Andean community of Choquechampi. Completion of this deep mountain ravine reservoir involved construction of a sixty-five-foot-high, 350-foot-long earthen levee to hold the rainwater that flows down surrounding mountains into the natural ravine. The community donated a portion of its public land for this project. The ravine's clay-bottom terrain helps prevent water from seeping into the ground below. Gravity-fed distribution channels, with a series of manually operated gates, direct the water throughout the surrounding fields, allowing farmers to irrigate over 300 hectares (741 acres) and providing water to more than 3,000 people who had not had sufficient water access.

Municipal officials and community leaders approached MMNM, requesting to partner with them to construct the project. Choquechampi's municipal engineers completed the feasibility study and initial design for the reservoir and projected its costs. Both the municipality and the community residents agreed to contribute the majority of the funds. Mano a Mano contributed its heavy machinery and a smaller portion of the funding.

As with all Mano a Mano projects, community residents provided the unskilled labor, which proved particularly daunting for this project. Because the bottom of the ravine was too narrow to accommodate heavy machines, residents and MMNM staff built by hand the knee wall—a short wall less than three feet in height—for the reservoir. They passed rocks from one to the other in fire-brigade fashion; mixed cement in a manual mixer; and pushed large stones across planks to create a 330-foot-thick wall that could support the weight of 700,000 cubic meters of water.

During the six months required to complete the knee wall, enthusiastic residents appeared every morning to complete one

more day of backbreaking work that would lead them to water. When the wall was complete, they celebrated with *chicha* (a
fermented beverage made from corn) and a brass band. Then,
as they watched the machines begin to fill the area behind the
wall, they protested. "Where will the water be?" they cried. At
that point the MMNM staff realized that, in spite of their presentation of the reservoir drawings during a community meeting, the residents had not understood how the project would
function. They thought the entire project was finished when
only the first phase had been completed. The residents' sense
of common purpose and camaraderie had deflated, but they
continued to contribute their labor and MMNM completed the
project.

When the completed reservoir began to collect water several months later, the community's enthusiasm revived. Residents
declared that they could see more water at the bottom of their
reservoir than they had ever seen in their lives. They quickly
dug the earthen channels through which water flows to their
crops and released small amounts of water to see how far it
would reach. Then they celebrated again, this time by using the
reservoir for baptisms.

The Choquechampi reservoir stands as a stunning and
highly functional Mano a Mano project. It is the most complex
design Mano a Mano has devised to date, and the most demand-
ing of community labor. Unfortunately, the cost of the project
exceeded the municipality's projections. MMNM chose to complete the project anyway, not wanting to leave the community
with an unfinished and useless construction. It renegotiated the
partnership agreement to increase the municipal contribution.
However, the municipality had no additional funds available
until the following year, having already devoted almost its entire annual infrastructure budget to this project. Consequently,
MMNM stretched itself very thin to cover the cost while continuing with other commitments. While the delayed payment
caused MMNM cash flow difficulties in the short term, in the

long term it fully recovered the monies owed by the municipality and learned some useful lessons.

When MMNM completes a water project, it helps local farmers form a water cooperative if they do not already have one. The cooperative schedules water releases, sets fees for water use, and maintains the reservoir.

In contrast to geographical areas in which MMNM has constructed large water reservoirs as a means to make water available for subsistence farmers, other areas require a different approach. Where farmers' one- to two-acre plots are dispersed around mountainsides rather than being contiguous as in communities such as Choquechampi, the small retention pond concept is a viable alternative.

Retention ponds serve up to four individual families. Although ponds may be located on the farmer's plot itself, they are more commonly positioned on a nearby section of the currently untilled mountainside. Each pond is located at the bottom of a natural collection point. The pond's exact location is determined by the MMNM engineer and farmers, who work together and consider the unique topography of each farm plot and the natural flow of rainwater. Ponds measure 120 by 120 feet and hold an average of 1,500 cubic meters of water. In addition to irrigating crops, ponds provide water for the family's personal needs and for their livestock.

## The Challenges of Agricultural Water Projects

Taking on the responsibility for constructing these complex infrastructure projects presents serious challenges. There is a storied history of desperation for water access in the region. Municipalities must ensure the security of sites from those who don't yet grasp the complex engineering and may interpret the efforts of MMNM as efforts to keep water from their families. This desperation is understandable.

Residents of several communities in which Mano a Mano

has completed reservoir projects had attempted to harness water unsuccessfully for decades. In one instance, in an attempt to enlarge a small reservoir, residents weakened the levee wall. During the next heavy rain, the wall burst and flooded the village, destroying most of its homes. In another, farmers with picks and shovels tried to dig a channel high along the mountainside through which spring water could flow down the mountain toward their fields. Instead, they loosened soil and rock and created a landslide that redirected the water away from them. Knowing of these previous accidents, MMNM staff requests that community leaders watch over the construction site to ensure that no one risks the safety of the community or the project while attempting to redirect or extract water.

*Each project requires a distinct engineering design.* In contrast to clinic or school construction projects that can be replicated in dozens of locations, water projects must be designed to fit the topography of each community in order to maximize water retention potential.

Water project designs vary considerably—from large lake-like reservoirs built on a flat basin to deep ravine reservoirs with a levee at one end to a round water pond dug into the side of a mountain. In some cases, water flows into the reservoir from a river. Others depend on high-altitude channels to feed spring water, snowmelt, and rain into the reservoir. Each project's cost, timeline, and water-flow analysis must be addressed in a unique engineering design.

*Living conditions for machine operators.* When operators move heavy machinery to a new project, they prepare to stay in the community for several months. In that period, these operators often take only one break to visit their families. Living for weeks at a time in these rural areas, they encounter harsh living conditions. Local volunteers offer to cook for them each day, but often have so little food available that operators cannot maintain a healthy diet. Lack of housing means they must sleep in tents, and cold mountain air and high altitude adds to their discomfort.

*Coordination with the municipality.* Bolivian law requires that the municipality complete a study of all proposed water projects' environmental impact, documentation of water source and flow, project design, and cost estimates. Road projects require similar studies. MMNM engineers review designs completed by municipal engineers and recommend any necessary changes. Given the Choquechampi experience with substantial underestimates of project costs, MMNM engineers now complete their own cost estimates and develop a common document with the municipality. The process can require many hours and numerous meetings until an agreement is reached, but this step is critical to ensure that projects can be completed within budgetary guidelines.

When MMNM begins a project, it moves heavy equipment to the site. Because this is costly, MMNM plans the location of each machine several months in advance. MMNM makes every attempt to keep projects moving forward once machines are in place. Municipalities, on the other hand, have limited annual budgets and a history of starting and stopping projects several times until they have funds to complete them. As a result, MMNM requires up-front payment of a portion of the municipal contribution during the budget year before the project begins, with the remainder due during a second year and third year, if necessary.

*Helping residents understand how the project functions.* Use of advanced, unfamiliar technology makes it difficult for residents to fully comprehend exactly how water will flow into the reservoir, how and where it will be held, and how to control its release. Lack of understanding created a serious problem a few weeks before MMNM completed the Laguna Sulti reservoir project. As heavy rains swelled the river that runs into the reservoir and water approached the top of the levee, a small group of farmers, working after dark, grabbed their picks and began to dig into the levee to release some of the water. In the morning other farmers discovered the damage and called the MMNM office. Staff rushed to the site and found that a three-foot length on top of the levee had been hacked open, compromising the levee. The damage resulted in water flowing over the wall, running along the levee base, and away from the fields. Community residents were furious over this vandalism. Before the MMNM staff arrived and demanded an explanation, they had identified the culprits. Those who damaged the wall said they saw water rising in the reservoir plus more flowing in from the river. They feared the water would overflow and flood their houses, as the river had done during heavy rains years ago, so they made sure their houses would be safe. These individuals had not understood that the river would overflow the other end of the levee before it could reach the top and then flow away as it always had.

*Disputes over water.* A simple question—Who owns the water?—nearly derailed MMNM's fourth reservoir project. Several years earlier, a European NGO initiated a water reservoir project for a municipality about thirty miles and several mountain ranges away from the community of Sancayani, with which MMNM had a signed agreement to complete a major reservoir project. After the other organization had completed the first phase of its project, it recognized that the water source it had identified was insufficient to meet projected need. The European NGO searched for and believed it had found additional water in large springs in the mountains above Sancayani. The organization began planning to reroute it. That decision led to a bitter conflict with the residents of Sancayani, who felt the water unquestionably belonged to them.

As an organization, MMNM has taken great care to ensure

that ownership issues do not derail projects—particularly water projects, given the history of violence over water in Bolivia. Throughout the planning and design phases of the Sancayani project, all partners felt confident that the water that would be channeled to the reservoir clearly belonged to the community of Sancayani. When the dispute arose, MMNM suspended construction and moved machinery to another project while the dispute was reviewed. While the issue was being resolved, municipal officials, the residents of Sancayani, and MMNM personnel managed the response admirably by providing information as needed and refusing to be intimidated by much more powerful constituencies. When the Bolivian national government ruled in favor of Sancayani, the project resumed.

As of early 2014, over 30,000 individuals benefit from MMNM agricultural water projects. The pride and gratitude of farm families inspire MMNM staff to continue this work in spite of the challenges. Mario Suarez, a municipal official, expressed a common sentiment: "Mano a Mano has fulfilled its part of the bargain 100 percent. Now we can continue the work and do even more."

## Road Projects

Lack of passable rural roads not only impedes access to health care, but also prevents farmers from transporting their produce to market. Bolivia's road infrastructure consists primarily of two-lane gravel roads that connect the country's principal cities to each other and minimal arterial dirt or gravel roads that lead to the main roads. Most rural residents of Bolivia's Andean departments (states) don't have access to even the most basic arterial roads and thus depend on llamas and donkeys to carry produce along mountain paths. Consequently, their families are isolated from Bolivia's social and economic structure with little hope of creating change. Most rural residents, who survive on less than a dollar a day, recognize that passable roads are the key to improved economic well-being. Many rural Bolivian municipalities have begun to allocate the majority of their annual budgets to water and road projects to address these needs. Their funding, however, is rarely able to cover more than one-third the cost of such projects.

In 2005, members of the rural El Palmar community traveled for twelve hours overnight on horseback to meet with Mano a Mano Bolivia personnel. El Palmar residents implored our staff to assist with a road project for which they had been unsuccessfully seeking funds for thirty years. "There are no roads in the entire El Palmar region, only paths for horses. Even a motorcycle, a bicycle, would be of no use here. We feel like we are living inside a corral. The only way we can get our crops to market is in the bellies of our hogs," said Don Cecilio, a community leader.

The program manager, who subsequently visited the area, confirmed Cecilio's concerns. He found produce rotting in the field because farmers had no means to transport it to market. He recommended that Mano a Mano help the community address the problem.

Up to this point, MMB had used heavy equipment to convert pathways into usable roads, but had not forged new roads. Accepting this request marked a major jump in project complexity. Personnel seriously considered the risks involved in signing an agreement that committed the organization to carve a solid roadway through tropical mountains. Could they estimate costs with confidence? Would their machinery withstand the increased demand for heavy performance? Did they have sufficient confidence in the municipality's engineering capacity to follow its specifications?

MMB agreed to complete the road project. Shortly after the agreement was signed, MMNM, the newly incorporated organization, took responsibility for the project. Ivo Velásquez, Segundo's brother, had worked with Mano a Mano from its earliest days on construction projects, contributing his exceptional carpentry and engineering skills. In his new capacity as an MMNM board member, he agreed to supervise construction of the Pilcomayo to Palmar Road and to manage all of MMNM's other road and water projects going forward.

Beginning in 2005, MMNM used its heavy equipment in partnership with rural municipalities to construct solid gravel roads that could support truck transport. Community residents participate in these projects, using their picks and shovels to build and grade protective sidewalls, channels, and culverts to redirect water and prevent damage to road surfaces. Just like the cost-effective method Mano a Mano depends on to build community facilities, the approach to road projects starts with community involvement.

Communities identify the need and make a request to partner with MMNM on a project. Municipal officials must agree to participate as a partner and contribute thirty to thirty-five percent of the project funding. MMNM negotiates an agreement governing the roles and responsibilities of each partner. Community residents agree to volunteer all unskilled labor required to complete the project. MMNM supervises and implements the project and provides the heavy equipment and skilled labor, while Mano a Mano U.S. provides oversight and a portion of the funding. Finally, with a formal dedication ceremony, MMNM turns the project over to the community and municipality.

Though the El Palmar road project was a daunting prospect for Mano a Mano Bolivia, MMNM's most challenging project to date came later. Residents of an agricultural region in the Cochabamba Valley told MMNM staff that they had been requesting help for twenty-eight years to build a road that would connect their communities to the high-altitude Uyuni mining region. Having access to the mining region would enable hundreds of farmers to tap into a new market. It would also mean 6,000 family members of the miners, who survived on food transported great distances, would have access to fresher produce and the possibility of better health. Two communities would connect for their mutual benefit.

The project required constructing a twenty-two-kilometer road on which trucks could safely carry full loads of produce across steep mountains. The road from Cotagaita to Uyuni, as contemplated, would begin at 8,500 feet above sea level and arrive at the mining community of Uyuni at an elevation of 16,500 feet. Having already completed 560 kilometers of rural roads, the staff felt confident that it could take on this extremely difficult project.

Equipment crews and community volunteers worked from opposite ends of the road. When they finally joined their completed sections, they sat down to share a celebration meal. They were astonished as a motorcycle and then a truck passed. "Where did they come from? How could they know we have finished?" asked the machine operators in disbelief.

The community volunteers told them, "Tomorrow there will be buses. Now Cotagaita is truly a part of Bolivia."

This ribbon-like road has reduced transport travel time to the mines from fifteen hours to one hour. With their lifelong dream of a road connection now a reality, farmers have new access to the miners and have begun to plant and harvest grapes and other marketable fruits and vegetables for their new customer base. The road has been a win-win for everyone, increasing Cotagaita farmers' incomes while improving the diet of Uyuni miners.

## Challenges Presented by Road Projects

These complex infrastructure projects present several of the same steep construction challenges as the water reservoir projects. They require unique and complex designs, engineering coordination with the municipality, municipal funding that spans more than one budget year, and efforts to maintain the morale of machine operators who live for extended periods in undesirable conditions, apart from their families. The results of these projects more than offset these challenges, however.

As the road grader completed the first two kilometers of the thirty-two-kilometer Palmar Road, the operator looked back, astonished to see a truck following behind him, already loading produce to haul to market. With tearing eyes, the community resident, who months before had pleaded for this road, said, "Now the doors to our corral are opening after generations of being closed. Now we can get materials to build better houses and schools and bring in teachers to educate our children. Now we are part of Bolivia."

Hector Arce, the mayor of Omereque, commented on a similar road project in his municipality: "Dozens of local volunteers using picks, shovels, machetes, and axes cleared trees and brush. Behind them the surveyor marked the roadbed. Then came the bulldozer, carving its way into the hillside, then the excavator, the dump trucks, and finally the road grader. The scene reminded me of an ant colony with its highly organized structure, each focused on its task and determined to follow its path. Now that farmers have a road, they can plant more crops because they can transport what their families don't eat and sell it in city markets."

## Airstrips

Together, MMB and MMNM have constructed airstrips in twenty-one communities where air travel would have otherwise been impossible. The airstrips open these areas up, not only to Mano a Mano, but also to government officials who were previously oblivious to the conditions of their people and to businessmen who may have had little contact with the area and were unaware of its development potential.

After it had an airstrip, the community of San Agustín decided to sponsor a trade fair. The community invited elected officials from other municipalities and representatives from

133

businesses throughout the region to sample the tea they produce from locally grown herbs. Leaders attributed the large attendance at the fair to the access the airstrip now provides, and expressed confidence that it will result in expanded markets for their tea.

## Lessons Learned from MMNM Projects

*Apply the basic Mano a Mano model to larger-scale, more complex economic development projects.*

*Examine project design specifications and cost estimates in detail.* Municipal engineers produce both documents, but do not assume responsibility for delivering the project within budget. MMNM now double-checks the municipality's designs and estimates to avoid cost over-runs and design flaws.

*Create project budgets that span more than one municipal fiscal year.* Water and road projects require much larger budget allocations and many more workdays to complete than do clinics or schools. Construction nearly always spans at least two and sometimes three fiscal years.

*Track compliance with maintenance agreements.* Although municipalities agree to maintain the roads, their maintenance may be inadequate. While some municipalities have followed through on their agreements to maintain roads constructed in partnership with Mano a Mano, others have not. Currently, Mano a Mano is developing a plan to periodically inspect previously constructed roads and to partner with municipalities to develop and follow a maintenance schedule. For future projects, MMNM has revised construction designs to reduce roads' ongoing maintenance needs.

*Plan for extensive inspections.* To ensure consistently high quality, every MMNM project is inspected according to a pre-determined plan or on an as-needed basis. Roads and water projects receive dozens of inspections during construction and regularly thereafter.

◆ ◆ ◆ ◆

MMNM was created to fulfill community requests to build the basic infrastructure necessary for rural economic development—water that leads to food security and roads that lead to urban markets. Desperate farmers articulate these needs when they approach MMNM. "Build a road with us and open the gates of the corral in which we live," one said. "Help us become a part of the country that is Bolivia." Others have said, "Water is life. We cannot live without water." As an organization, MMNM responds to these appeals to create opportunities for those who live in Bolivia's marginalized communities.

(left) Mano a Mano in the early years; co-founder Segundo Velásquez picking up donated medical supplies with his trailer.

(below) Supplies were stored in two make-shift tents in Joan and Segundo's backyard for many years.

Donated medical supplies and equipment arriving at a new clinic in Tica Pampa.

Mano a Mano volunteers load wheelchairs during a container shipment from the Mano a Mano warehouse in Eagan, MN in 2008.

A child in Bolivia receiving a donated wheelchair from Mano a Mano in December 2013.

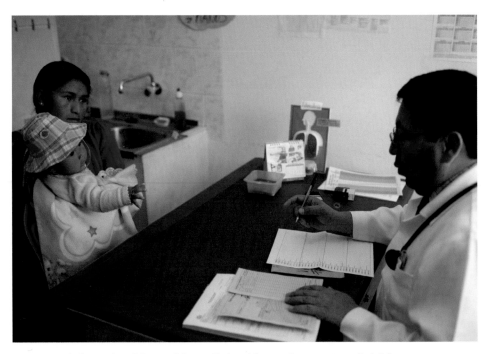

A doctor in a Mano a Mano clinic with a patient; maternal-child care is one of the primary focus areas in Mano a Mano clinics.

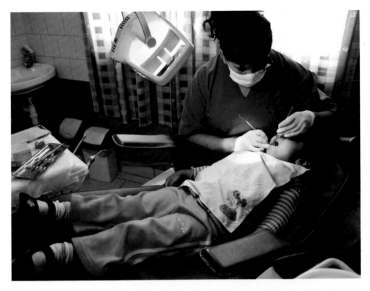

Dental care is a large emphasis in Mano a Mano clinics; more than 20 percent of all patient visits are for dental care, and 16 percent of Mano a Mano medical professionals on staff are dentists.

In every clinic, an average of ten community residents are trained as volunteer health promoters.

One of the 501 emergency air rescues in 2013; a newborn child in Oruro who encountered complications shortly after birth had to be transported to Cochabamba for immediate treatment. The flight took thirty minutes, as opposed to five-six hours. The child survived.

A Mano a Mano education project in Chilijchi, Bolivia—housing for teachers.

Schoolchildren in Mano a Mano's school in Apote, Bolivia.

Every project begins with a community request and a meeting with Mano a Mano staff;
Mano a Mano Bolivia Executive Director José Velásquez meets
with community leaders about a proposed project.

Ivo Velásquez showing residents of Laguna Sulti the design of their
water project. Mano a Mano staff holds regular meetings with
every community throughout the process.

Mano a Mano Nuevo Mundo Project Director Ivo Velásquez stopping by a resident's home in Sancayani during a site visit for the water reservoir built there.

Mano a Mano's water reservoir project in Sancayani, Bolivia, 14,000 feet above sea level.

Laguna Sulti resident Don Primitivo excited to see the water pumping from the Mano a Mano reservoir built in his community.

A typical community Mano a Mano works with is high in the Andes, and residents have small plots of land for subsistence farming, like the community of Rodeo in the municipality of Icla.

Aerial view of Mano a Mano's sixty kilometer road project in El Palmar, connecting communities to roads for the first time.

Trucks passing through on a newly completed section of road in El Palmar, Bolivia.

Sancayani residents volunteering on their water reservoir project
preparing the levee for cobblestones.

Dedications of new projects are always a big event; the community, Mano a Mano staff, and visitors
from the U.S. march to their newly completed project in Chiro K'asa in the department of Potosi.

# 8

# Training and Outreach

*Mano a Mano Internacional is simply an astounding organi-*
*zation; they make every visitor feel immediately welcomed*
*and valued in the office, on the road, and at the CEA. Every*
*detail of a trip is taken care of and tailored to visitors' needs,*
*and the staff makes sure that it is impossible not to be*
*smiling for the entire visit.*
**—Samantha Carter, Mano a Mano U.S. office intern who**
**traveled to Bolivia during the summer of 2013**[56]

Sometimes an unfulfilled opportunity has unintended con-
sequences. A U.S. mining company contact approached
Segundo and Dan Narr, executive director of Mano a Mano
U.S., in 2012 about the mining company's business interests in
Bolivia and its related desire to donate to Mano a Mano. The
mining executive indicated that he didn't want to focus on a
specific project, but wished to move forward with a donation.
He insisted that any donation go directly to a Bolivian NGO.
Just as the parties were set to finalize the details, the mining
company official received word that he had been transferred to
Mongolia. The donation did not materialize.

It was this unsolicited, but failed, fundraising effort that set

Mano a Mano on the path toward the formation of a fourth Bolivian counterpart. Mano a Mano proposed that the new organization, incorporated in Bolivia as an NGO, would concentrate on fundraising and seek funding within Bolivia from embassies, foreign businesses, and other organizations. We believed their local fundraising efforts would be useful to all three existing counterpart organizations in Bolivia.

Mano a Mano Bolivia (MMB), Mano a Mano Neuvo Mundo (MMNM), and Mano a Mano Apoyo Aéreo (MMAA) all operate independently. While they retain close ties to Mano a Mano U.S. and coordinate with us and each other, they maintain a significant degree of autonomy. This new organization, we anticipated, would maintain closer ties to Mano a Mano U.S. The Mano a Mano U.S. board believed the new organization might serve, in some sense, as Mano a Mano's main office in Bolivia for coordination purposes.

Though the original impetus for the formation of a fourth Bolivian NGO centered on fundraising, by the time the organizational documents were drafted the reasons for its existence and the strategies for its role had evolved.

## Creating a New Organization, Mano a Mano Internacional

In 2012, Mano a Mano took steps to formalize the structure and legal status of this fourth Bolivian counterpart organization, called Mano a Mano Internacional (MMI). Organized as an NGO, MMI is a small organization based in Cochabamba. Its director is María Blanca Velásquez, Segundo's sister. MMI also employs a secretary and an on-staff agronomist. Its offices are in a residential building that members of the Velásquez family built. In this sense, the organization's trajectory is like that of other Mano a Mano entities. At start-up, it adopted a step-by-step, make-do approach that minimized overhead costs.

Persuasive arguments for creating this entity included the

advantage of having a single entity in Bolivia intent on fund-raising, communications, hosting travelers, and developing pilot programs that might affect any or all of Mano a Mano's other Bolivian counterparts. Mano a Mano's U.S. board created MMI to achieve the following goals:

- Establish positive contacts with the U.S. Embassy and Consuls, U.S. government agencies (such as USAID), and U.S. corporations that conduct business in Bolivia.

- Solicit funds from foreign embassies, businesses, NGOs, and other potential donors to Mano a Mano programs in Bolivia.

- Enhance communication between Bolivian counterpart organizations and Mano a Mano U.S. by providing or arranging translation services (Spanish/English) and preparing informational materials.

- Create, organize, and coordinate excellent experiences in Bolivia for volunteers, potential funders, and other visitors from the United States.

- Complete feasibility assessments and pilot new programs (e.g., training in sustainable agriculture) at the request of Mano a Mano U.S.

- Develop the organizational structure required to function effectively in Bolivia in a manner consistent with both Bolivian and U.S. laws and regulations.

## MMI's First-Year Accomplishments

In January 2013, the Bolivian government gave final approval of MMI's bylaws and its NGO status. But even before it had this official status, the new organization was able to prove its value through the achievement of some significant objectives. During its first year, MMI laid the groundwork for future operations through a substantial set of accomplishments.

Consistent with the original rationale for its existence, MMI prepared major fundraising proposals and delivered these proposals to embassies, businesses located in Bolivia, and foreign NGOs. So far the response has been limited, but it is too early to assess the value of these preliminary fundraising initiatives.

MMI also managed the processing of four containers loaded with items donated in the United States, and distributed these items to Mano a Mano's other counterparts. In recent years, Mano a Mano's distribution program has expanded from almost exclusively medical supplies to construction and repair equipment, school supplies, and supplies on behalf of other nonprofit organizations (who pay Mano a Mano for these shipments, which helps subsidize our container costs). When donated supplies are sent in mixed batches, it has proved useful to have an on-site NGO director take responsibility for sorting the shipped items and distributing them appropriately.

For sixteen years, Mano a Mano has arranged trips for volunteers and donors who want to see the clinics, schools, roads, and reservoirs the organization has built. The on-site management of these trips, which is time consuming, has always been a hurdle. Now MMI has assumed this responsibility. During its first year, MMI managed trips to Bolivia for twenty-nine groups from the United States and Europe. About half of these groups traveled to volunteer their time to a project. The other half were there to see Mano a Mano projects firsthand and consider a donation to our work.

Mano a Mano volunteers come to Bolivia from all over the

world. In the past, Mano a Mano U.S. and Mano a Mano Bolivia have shared responsibility for hosting and coordinating these groups and individuals. Those responsibilities have now shifted to MMI. Two groups of Oxford students were among the first volunteers to arrive under the new arrangement.

MMI was also tasked with developing and piloting new projects. Even prior to 2013, María Blanca Velásquez, Segundo's sister, had assisted with pilot projects instituted by Mano a Mano U.S. She continues to do so in her capacity as MMI's director. What started as an add-on function for MMI has already assumed considerable significance. One pilot project in 2011 took advantage of Mano a Mano's partnership with the University of Minnesota through its Humphrey School. Through this partnership, the Humphrey School's top-ranked program in nonprofit management offered its students an opportunity for not-for-profit field work in Bolivia.

Mano a Mano worked with the Humphrey School to organize and implement the students' on-site participation in a Bolivian agricultural study project. The project followed up on an MMNM project constructing water retention structures. One element of the study required the students to interview twenty Bolivian farmers who had benefited from the retention ponds. Given the terrain and how the farmers were dispersed, the assignment was more challenging than the Humphrey School students expected. To conduct the interviews, the students walked as much as four hours from one farmer's home to another. As requested by Mano a Mano U.S., María Blanca set up the interviews and accompanied the students.

The results of the interviews were instructive. Following the harvest of their primary crop (usually potatoes), the farmers were able to plant certain garden-variety vegetables for the first time. The students learned that happenstance had brought the farmers a supply of seeds. A Bolivian agronomist (unrelated to Mano a Mano), traveling from one rural village to another, had come through the municipality of Omereque, where he stopped at each farm along the way and provided each farmer he met with vegetable seeds. The farmers planted the seeds and waited for the fruit to appear. It was a learning experience. But the Bolivian farmers had never seen broccoli before and didn't know when or how to harvest it.

In response to the Humphrey students' interview questions, the farmers asked for training. "Teach us," they requested. Responding to the farmers' requests, Mano a Mano obtained funding for workshops. With targeted funds and under the direction of the U.S. board, MMI created a training center and demonstration garden in Cochabamba and organized the requested training. Over the summer of 2013, the MMI training center enrolled its first group of Bolivian farmers. With the MMI agronomist as an advisor and instructor, they responded to farmers' requests for training in best maintenance practices for: water projects; maximizing the use of water; sound agricultural practices for the selection, planting, and rotation of crops for Bolivia's soil and weather conditions; minimizing soil erosion; natural control of pests and the use of natural fertilizer; cultivating fruits and vegetables never grown before, but shown to thrive in Bolivia's environment; raising animals to improve the family diet while minimizing the spread of disease; preparing and preserving fruits, vegetables, and meat in ways that would improve the family diet throughout the year; and packaging and marketing agricultural products for sale. During the spring 2013 semester, the training center also provided internships for twenty-five Bolivian agronomy students.

Malnutrition is persistent and widespread in rural Bolivia. In pursuit of its mission to improve health, Mano a Mano considers the operation of the MMI training center to be the next logical step for improving nutrition and teaching Bolivian farmers best practices to maximize the impact of their water projects.

# 9

# Fundraising as a Linchpin of Success

*We were looking for a partner with a track record of perfor-*
*mance. This reservoir offers 600 families a chance to lift them-*
*selves out of poverty. We view this as economic*
*development; we don't treat it as charity at all.*
**—Valdi Stefanson, Rotarian from St. Paul, Minnesota**

For virtually every nonprofit organization, fundraising is imperative. What may seem like a relatively low priority at
start-up becomes increasingly critical.

Large organizations may hire professional fundraisers or
employ a staff member whose primary responsibility is fundraising. During its first ten years of operation (1994–2004),
Mano a Mano did not exercise either of these options. Consistent with its overall step-by-step, measured approach to its
mission, Mano a Mano proceeded cautiously where funding
was a concern. It stuck to its tight budget, relied on volunteer
labor, and conserved its limited resources. While Mano a Mano
has always sought in-kind donations whenever possible, actual

dollars are also essential. Of all the tasks required to establish Mano a Mano as a viable organization, fundraising proved the most elusive.

Each development phase required a different approach. While fundraising efforts may seem obvious and easy in retrospect, fundraising was for Mano a Mano neither evident nor effortless at any stage. Each step required research and hours of discussion. It involved many lunch and dinner meetings, phone calls, grant proposals, and reports.

At start-up, Mano a Mano's medical supply program was a relatively low-cost venture that depended on volunteer labor in Minnesota and Bolivia. But, as Mano a Mano's mission and programs expanded to include construction high in the Andes, its need for funds increased dramatically. Raising funds to support all of the organization's programs remains a primary responsibility of Mano a Mano's U.S. office. While the fundraising tools and sources have evolved over time, the organization has, since its inception, followed a basic seven-step framework in its approach to donors and prospective donors.

## Identifying, Attracting, and Retaining Funders

*Raise awareness of specific needs in Bolivia.* Mano a Mano integrates statistics on the status of health and economic development alongside stories about individuals into all of its presentations and materials.

*Identify prospective funders.* Mano a Mano searches foundation databases, reviews public IRS documents from other organizations, and talks with hundreds of individuals to search out foundations, businesses, and persons who might donate.

*Inform prospective funders.* Mano a Mano gathers information regarding a donor's philanthropic focus, previous donations, and current interests. When a donor's interests align with Mano a Mano's programs, Mano a Mano personnel emphasize this common interest and customize materials presented to that donor. They stress the essential components of Mano a Mano's community-based model and its demonstrated successes with already-completed projects in Bolivia. Mano a Mano's track record of successful and sustainable projects becomes part of every conversation and every proposal.

*Ask for the donation.* Mano a Mano adapts our request to the situation. It may involve a formal grant proposal that lays out background on Mano a Mano and a project's particular purpose, goals, methods, budget, and benefits to the funding entity. Alternatively, the request for a donation may be delivered in person during a meeting or dinner.

*Thank and recognize donors.* Mano a Mano provides a prompt thank you for every donation received, usually within a week. Mano a Mano regularly recognizes donors for the difference their generosity makes in the lives of rural Bolivians.

*Allocate funds and track performance.* Funds are allocated based on balancing community requests with available resources. Mano a Mano's U.S. board and staff match project requests with the interests of donors. The majority of individual donors and essentially all foundations specify the types of project they will consider funding. After Mano a Mano receives and allocates funds, it closely tracks project performance and keeps the donor informed.

*Update and involve donors* on the difference their funds are making in the lives of rural Bolivians. Mano a Mano communicates with donors through the donor's preferred medium—formal reports, letters, photos, phone calls, lunch and dinner meetings, and visits to Mano a Mano's Minnesota office. We've found that a mix of quantitative data and personal stories is preferable.

Mano a Mano's fundraising principles, which embody a thoughtful and conscientious approach to donor relationships, have served us well. Though the underlying precepts have stayed the same, Mano a Mano's fundraising efforts have differed with each phase of our growth.

## Phase I (1994–96)

Phase I focused on incorporating the organization and implementing a program to distribute donated U.S. medical surplus in Bolivia. This phase required minimal funds. To minimize our dependence on monetary donations, we searched for every opportunity to avoid spending money, relying heavily on volunteers and in-kind donations. Mano a Mano had no paid staff in Bolivia until 1998 (year five) and none in the U.S. until 2004 (year eleven). Volunteers took on all work of the organization in both countries until we hired staff. Even during Phase I, Mano a Mano received donated medical items, the value of which totaled hundreds of thousands of dollars, but managed the substantial inventory without paid help. In Minnesota, Segundo and I provided no-cost office and storage space. The Bolivian founders did the same. In the United States, our personal vehicles and trailer transported all medical donations at no cost. Cargo shipping costs were covered almost entirely by the Denton Program.

At first, Mano a Mano sent ninety-nine percent of all funds raised to Bolivia, making it possible for the organization to initiate its clinic program, distribute medical donations, and support volunteers there. While this approach held appeal for many donors, however, Mano a Mano found that over the long run this level of frugality was not sustainable.

## Funding Distribution of Medical Surplus

To raise funds to cover the organization's very modest initial expenses, board members compiled a list of donation approaches they thought might be effective. Based on that simple list, the organization created a plan with three components.

*Direct-mail appeal.* We identified groups of people who might be interested in donating because of a personal relationship or because they appeared to have a strong tie to Bolivia. Two different direct-mail letters were prepared and sent, one to family members and friends and one to members of the Asociación de Bolivianos en Minnesota. Almost all family and friends responded to the direct-mail plea with modest donations for a total of about $1,000. Only one of the Bolivian nationals on the Asociación mailing list donated, in the amount of twenty dollars. The lack of response from this Bolivian organization was deeply disappointing. Segundo had carefully crafted a Spanish appeal letter with help from one of the Asociación members and felt confident that the group would assist. Perhaps if Mano a Mano had proposed to work in any of the members' own hometowns, these individuals would have helped raise funds, contributed their time and dollars, and traveled to Bolivia to present the gifts in person.

*Sales of crafts.* A friend who owned a coffee house offered to set up a table of Bolivian crafts that his staff could sell on Mano a Mano's behalf. These sales raised several hundred dollars each year.

*Events.* A board member hosted the first event, a volunteer-prepared Bolivian dinner accompanied by Andean music performed by four Bolivian musicians. Mano a Mano charged $20 per guest, netted $2,000, and felt wealthy.

These fundraising efforts, coupled with extensive volunteer hours and creativity in obtaining in-kind donations, supported the organization's initial modest vision of donating medical surplus.

## Funding the First Two Community Clinics

In 1996, the board expanded its vision, intending to support the dream of creating a clinic program if the opportunity arose. The seventieth birthday party of Gloria MacRae provided that opportunity. Because Gloria did not want gifts, we decided to ask her friends secretly for donations to Mano a Mano. The initial goal was to raise sufficient funds to purchase a high-powered microscope or possibly an operating table for use in a Bolivian hospital. Eventually the Mano a Mano board settled on a risky but appealing idea: why not ask for funds for a satellite clinic that would be named Clínica Gloria?

A few days before the party, I received a call from the husband of one of Gloria's friends saying that an anonymous donor wished to contribute $5,000 to build the satellite clinic. With this gift and those from other friends, Mano a Mano raised $11,000 in honor of Gloria's landmark birthday. Our astonished Bolivian counterparts decided to use these funds as seed money. We raised enough additional funding in Bolivia to construct two satellite clinics.

The birthday party also presented a secondary fundraising opportunity. One month earlier, Segundo's employer had donated over 6,000 never-used cut-glass wine glasses, a gift too valuable to refuse. The party host, a board member, suggested giving one glass to each guest and then offering additional glasses for two dollars each. Guests cleaned out the inventory we brought to the party, and then Gloria assumed the role of super salesperson. Within a few months she had sold over 5,500 wine glasses.

Taking advantage of these serendipitous fundraising opportunities provided sufficient seed money for Mano a Mano to consider building more clinics if additional funding became available.

Throughout this early phase, we talked with donors and volunteers about Mano a Mano's achievements in Bolivia whenever possible. Every donor received an immediate formal thank-you letter, and donations above $500 triggered a personal thank-you phone call. In addition to these personal contacts, we wrote and sent three simple newsletters each year to donors of funds and medical supplies, volunteers, and other people who had expressed an interest in our organization and mission. The message remained consistent: Mano a Mano was a good steward of all donations and those donations made a very concrete and compelling difference in Bolivia.

## Sources of Funding

Compared to future phases, the funds we raised in Phase I were modest. Individuals provided the vast majority of the funding, with wine glass sales and a successful dinner event making up the rest. Mano a Mano neither applied for nor received foundation grants during this phase. Nor did we attempt to raise funds in Bolivia. Volunteers completed all of the work required and the medical group provided storage space for cargo that arrived from the United States. Friends and family members transported supplies and equipment to their destination at no cost and distributed them free of charge.

# Lessons Learned in Phase I

*Begin small.* Until Mano a Mano developed a successful track record, we had neither the potential funding sources nor the expertise to embark on a larger, more costly fundraising campaign.

*Seek donations of things, time, and talent.* The founders always thought first about where and how to obtain, at no cost, whatever the organization needed in order to function.

*Nurture relationships.* We communicated frequently with those who donated funds as well as with volunteers and donors of medical supplies. The message: your donation makes a difference and we are good stewards of your gifts.

*Don't depend on responses to mailed appeals.* Only family members and close friends responded.

*Remain nimble in order to take advantage of unanticipated opportunities.* A birthday party provided an opportunity to request donations and sell a popular donated item.

*Before raising funds, decide what they will be used for.* The board had already decided how to use additional funding long before anyone thought of a birthday party as a funding opportunity. With this priority in mind, we could build enthusiasm for a gift that would touch the hearts of Gloria's friends and inspire their generosity.

## Phase II (1997–2000)

Phase II brought even more ambitious goals. Mano a Mano resolved to construct and establish health-care programs in one or two community clinics yearly and distribute up to 150,000 pounds of donated medical surplus. Setting the bar so high required a new approach to raising funds. Until this point, fundraising had been on a very small scale. Mano a Mano had responded to the rapid growth in the medical supply program with modest increases in donated income. By the end of 1997, though, the U.S. board decided that the organization could no longer expect to operate without paid staff in Bolivia. The board decided to fund one full-time position and one part-time position and also add a line item to clinic construction budgets for master carpenter services.

While wrestling with the increased need for funds, the board began to seek donations from individual donors with a holiday gift letter inviting donors to "give the gift of giving." The donor could choose among various gifts to Mano a Mano such as "shipping 150 pounds of medical supplies to Bolivia" or "paying a nurse's salary for two weeks." Recipients received a hand-made gift card with traditional Bolivian designs from Mano a Mano letting them know that a donation had been made in their honor. Considering our small mailing list at the time, this appeal proved very successful. We received most of our individual donations during the holidays.

## Board Tackles the Increased Need for Funds

The board knew that Mano a Mano could not continue to depend on individual donors to support our growing organization, and we invited a professional fundraiser to join the board and help address the challenge. His relationship-based approach to fundraising fit well with Mano a Mano's personal style and his guidance proved to be invaluable. Initially, he reviewed the donor list and reminded board members of the anonymous $5,000 donation to the Gloria Clinic fund. Another board member offered to host a dinner party for the board, the most active volunteers, and the anonymous donor's liaison. After the meal, Segundo and I displayed graphs that showed the dramatic increase in medical donations from 1994 to 1997 and the impact of these donations on the hospital that received them and on the recently opened Gloria Clinics. The presentation was well received, and we were invited to prepare a funding request for the anonymous donor's foundation. That request resulted in a modest three-year funding commitment.

| Medical Surplus Program | 1994 | 1995 | 1996 | 1997 |
|---|---|---|---|---|
| Value of Medical Inventory | $1,787 | $64,308 | $176,977 | $190,000 |
| Value of Donated Transportation | $300 | $2,316 | $43,740 | $40,080 |
| Pounds of Medical Supplies Shipped to Bolivia | 500 | 3,000 | 67,000 | 107,000 |
| Clinics Constructed and Opened | - | - | - | 2 |

◆ ◆ ◆ ◆

The fundraiser who served on Mano a Mano's board encouraged us to develop a three-year fundraising plan that focused on foundations and companies doing business in Bolivia. With his expert guidance we learned the importance of the following lessons:

*Don't waste time sending dozens of proposals* to foundations or businesses before learning a lot about them. Search for foundations with which Mano a Mano shares common interests and companies that have a business interest in Bolivia.

*Read foundation and business websites* and any other available information carefully, and then contact their staff to discuss whether and how Mano a Mano fits their guidelines.

*Look for unusual connections* between a prospective donor and Mano a Mano. For example, several Mano a Mano volunteers were graduates of a college that received support from a Twin Cities foundation. Mano a Mano wrote up a grant proposal to this foundation. The founders took a group photo of these graduates and discussed in the proposal the college's influence on their decision to become involved in international work. This foundation awarded one of Mano a Mano's first grants.

*Prepare a proposal that speaks to a foundation's interests,* follows their outline, and responds to their questions. Prepare a budget consistent with the proposal and the foundation's grant range and requirements. Be clear about who will benefit from the requested funds, how they will benefit, and what activities and actions will be supported with their funding.

*Attend to detail.* Reread the proposal, budget, and all attachments for consistency, and correct any errors.

*Invite the foundation's staff to conduct a site visit of local facilities,* and respond immediately to any questions they raise about the proposal.

A graduate student enrolled in a grant-writing class volunteered to complete Mano a Mano's first foundation search. She located a foundation that funds international programs and helped prepare a proposal. The Christmas holidays came a day early that year when Mano a Mano received its first competitive foundation grant award. Winning the grant enhanced Mano a Mano's credibility when applying for other grants. After thorough research, we prepared proposals to two local foundations. The proposals were approved and provided significant support for Mano a Mano throughout Phase II. In preparing and submitting the proposals, we paid close attention to reporting requirements and reporting deadlines. Each of the three foundations continued to award yearly grants to Mano a Mano for several years beyond their customary three-year limit.

However, the search for support from businesses did not yield results. Relatively few Twin Cities companies do business in Bolivia. Those companies that do, we learned, did not have a philanthropic focus consistent with Mano a Mano's mission.

We reached our three-year funding goals primarily by identifying potential foundation donors, crafting proposals that
appealed specifically to their interests, achieving projected results, paying meticulous attention to the preparation of reports,
and submitting these reports on time.

## Sources of Funding

During Phase II, our fundraising efforts increased significantly.
By 2000, our yearly funding had increased more than tenfold.
Foundation grants accounted for fifty-seven percent of contributions and individuals for thirty-seven percent of total funding
during Phase II. We did not receive funds from businesses or
corporations.

When Mano a Mano raised funds to construct Clínica Gloria, the medical group with whom we were collaborating
decided to use this funding as seed money. The group matched
the donated amount and built two clinics with assistance from
Mano a Mano and villagers who would ultimately use its services. This decision established a precedent that Mano a Mano
has followed since then.

We do not take on a project unless a portion of the funding is made available by Bolivian sources. During this phase we
built one or two clinics yearly, managed their health care and
education programs and funded their staff salaries. Municipalities contributed modest amounts of funding, some furnishings,
and electricity. Community residents provided locally available
materials (sand, for example), the lot for the building site, and
all unskilled labor. On average, these contributions covered ten
to fifteen percent of the total project cost.

## Lessons Learned in Phase II

*Seek advice from a professional* who is willing to assist on a pro
bono basis. Although our fundraising lessons may seem obvi-

ous in retrospect, they were not obvious at the time.

*Tell your story to persons who have shown interest.* The dinner party proved to be an excellent medium for conversation about Mano a Mano, followed by a brief and to-the-point presentation.

*Follow personal relationships.* Potential donors are more likely to respond to someone they know than to a cold call.

*Be creative with volunteer assignments.* Upon learning of the Mano a Mano volunteer who was enrolled in a grant-writing course, I suggested she switch assignments. At my suggestion, she no longer spent her volunteer hours sorting medical supplies. Instead she compiled a list of foundations and wrote up a proposal that won Mano a Mano a sizeable grant. This resourceful adjustment resulted in a true win-win situation. The student experienced the thrill of meaningful success, and Mano a Mano reaped the benefit of receiving its first foundation grant beyond our anonymous donor.

*Do a thorough investigation* of each prospective foundation or business and tailor the proposal to its unique interests and guidelines. I sometimes cut and pasted sections from one proposal to another, but I never simply copied one proposal to submit to other potential donors.

*Pay careful attention to foundation granting and reporting requirements.* Respond to questions and do not miss deadlines.

## Phase III (2001–04)

By 2000, Mano a Mano's medical supply program was operating smoothly. By the end of Phase II, Mano a Mano had built five rural clinics in addition to those first two peri-urban clinics (Clínica Gloria I and Clínica Gloria II). In addition, we had made preparations for the thirty-clinic project. Mano a Mano had not yet built any schools. During Phase III, we focused first on raising funds to build more community clinics. By the end of this phase we had added schools, housing for teachers, and sanitation projects to our expanding list of projects.

## Funding Expansion of the Community Clinic Program

The growth in both the medical surplus and health-clinic programs led the board to attempt a new fundraising strategy. We set out to strengthen donor involvement through increasing a donor's firsthand knowledge about the impact of Mano a Mano's projects in Bolivia. The founders invited a major donor contact and several devoted volunteers to travel to Bolivia where they could spend ten days seeing Mano a Mano projects in person and visit popular tourist sites.

After one such trip, the donor contact asked us to prepare a complete proposal with two budgets for presentation to the individual we had come to think of as the anonymous donor. One requested proposal set out projected costs to build thirty clinics and the other to build eighty clinics. Mano a Mano requested and received a planning grant from this donor to cover planning-related expenses. The anonymous donor ultimately approved the thirty-clinic proposal, with the understanding that Mano a Mano would request funding for another fifty clinics if the project proved successful.

Mano a Mano U.S. worked closely with MMB to set up the necessary infrastructure and monitoring systems and to safeguard funds. Mano a Mano U.S. maintained almost daily contact with MMB and reviewed the quarterly reports of its activities and expenditures. Mano a Mano U.S. then submitted quarterly reports to the anonymous donor, who would release the next quarter's funding. In addition to these reports, we met frequently with the anonymous donor's intermediaries to review program accomplishments and any issues of special concern. We also prepared lengthy annual performance reports.

## Soliciting Funds for Education Infrastructure Projects

When MMB began to receive requests for schools and housing for teachers in early 2002, the Mano a Mano U.S. board decided to support this expansion if it could raise the necessary funds. I successfully applied for several foundation grants to build sanitation projects, classrooms, and teacher housing. For each of these grants I sought guidance from the foundation's program officer regarding the focus of the proposal and the amount requested. These conversations not only helped me shape proposals but often resulted in suggestions of other foundations to which Mano a Mano might apply.

The program officer for a local foundation that had supported Mano a Mano programs for several years called me to suggest that Mano a Mano submit a proposal to a newly formed family foundation. I phoned the new foundation's officer, who described the foundation's focus, board members' interests, and their approach to what percentage of a project budget their foundation would fund. Based on the information I gathered from the phone call, I decided to apply for funds to build a school in one of the communities on the waiting list. Because this foundation usually chose to fund between twenty-five and fifty-five percent of a project budget, I included in the budget funds that individual donors had restricted to building schools. The foundation awarded Mano a Mano the amount requested, and continued to fund projects each year for several more years until its board said that it had already violated its "fund one organization for a maximum of three years" rule, and could not continue to ignore its own policies. Unfortunately, Mano a Mano had reached this point with several foundations when the 2008 financial crisis occurred and made the arduous task of raising funds even more difficult.

## Implementing Donor Visits as a Fundraising Strategy

Recognizing that travel to Bolivia to see Mano a Mano projects firsthand had cemented the anonymous donor's long-term support, Segundo began to organize other tours for small groups of interested persons. One of these trips, which included a volunteer fluent in Spanish, opened a door to new possibilities. We established a small contract with this volunteer to write a newsletter and lead an additional annual trip for five to twelve travelers to Bolivia.

Travelers helped move furniture into new clinics and schools and participated in project dedications. They had opportunities to interact with the rural Bolivians who had worked so hard to bring these projects to completion and with dedicated clinic staff. One wrote the following journal entry:

> As we approach the clinic, sitting under a huge shade tree are about eighty women and twice as many children under five years. It is women's day at the clinic, and they have come for their biweekly meeting. Half the group has been meeting for a year; the others are in a new group. Dr. Luisa Ramirez wants us to evaluate her work by asking questions of the women. If they have answers, we (and she) will know her work has been successful.
>
> The goal of the clinic is to reduce malnutrition to zero. With the help of better nutrition and government-supplied vitamins, malnutrition has already been reduced in one year. Some women have their children's growth charts with them. A colored piece of yarn is tied to the cards, and this indicates the level of growth.
>
> We ask questions like: "What foods have vitamin A?"
>
> "Carrots, they prevent blindness," they say.
>
> As we end our meeting under the tree, one woman says, "We have learned many things from the doctor."
>
> That is obvious. They also seem to respect and love her.

*Dr. Luisa speaks Spanish and Quechua. Public health education is her primary goal.*

*Inside the clinic, Dr. Luisa shows the scale model she has made of Charamoco. Little houses, the clinic, the school. She has put pins with different colored heads to indicate the number of babies, children ages one to five, six to ten, etc. On the wall are the charts of the children to track immunizations and growth. In the first year, vaccinations have gone from seven percent to ninety-three percent. "We'll get to 100 percent this year," says Dr. Luisa.*

Mano a Mano has led more than fifty trips to Bolivia. Most trips last from seven to ten days, with about half of the time devoted to seeing Mano a Mano projects and the rest getting to know Bolivia. All groups travel into Bolivia's rural areas and meet families who have benefited from Mano a Mano projects. After returning home, nearly all travelers expand their commitment of either volunteer time or funds.

## Sources of Funding

During Phase III, the amount of funds raised more than doubled. At this stage, the proportion of foundation grants as a source of funds increased to eighty-seven percent, reflecting our focus on preparing and submitting numerous foundation proposals and the sizable contribution from our anonymous donor. While individual donations also increased, they did not rise at the same rate.

When preparing a proposal to the anonymous donor in the fall of 2000, we made a far-reaching decision that had a profound impact on future expansion policies. Instead of funding all staff salaries in the expanding Mano a Mano clinic network, we would require that a Bolivian source cover the salary of either the physician or nurse as soon as the clinic opened and the second salary within three years. By the end of 2004, only eighteen of our 116 clinic staff were paid from Mano a Mano funds. We had far exceeded our original projections. We cannot over-emphasize the importance of this policy determination. Mano a Mano could not have continued to expand its clinic network while retaining the responsibility to pay clinic staff salaries.

## Lessons Learned in Phase III

*Keep donors informed* about the project they fund and the work of the organization. Segundo and I prepared lunches and dinners for individual donors to update them, answer their questions, and tell them stories of people who had directly benefited from their generous gifts. Only rarely did we request additional funding during these informal get-togethers.

*Encourage travel to Bolivia.* Words and photos do not substitute for viewing projects firsthand and meeting the proud and grateful beneficiaries.

*Do not sell the organization short.* It has been an ongoing struggle for Mano a Mano to balance its commitment to frugality with the reality that it takes resources to support the necessary administrative tasks. Because we contribute our time without remuneration and because the organization's offices were based in our home, initial normal administrative costs were extremely low. Bare-bones administrative funding became increasingly stressful with Mano a Mano's rapid growth. During Phase III, as paid staff members from Mano a Mano U.S. sometimes substituted for Segundo in conducting tours, the amount charged to travelers did not cover either their time away from everyday administrative responsibilities or their travel costs. This led to the decision to add those very real costs to the amount charged to travelers. Donors may be very impressed with startlingly low overhead costs or the ability to travel to Bolivia so inexpensively, but starving the organization of the resources to cover day-to-day operating costs does not foster its long-term sustainability.

## Phase IV (2005–Present)

By Phase IV, Mano a Mano needed to raise funds to: fuel the growth of our clinic and education infrastructure programs, make up any shortages in the operation of the aviation program, support economic development projects, and fund long neglected administrative needs in the United States. But from the start, Phase IV funding had a specific goal connected to a generous grant from our anonymous donor.

### Supporting Health and Education Infrastructure

Once Mano a Mano successfully demonstrated our ability to implement the goals of the anonymous donor's first grant for clinic construction, we were encouraged to submit a second, even more ambitious, funding request. We worked closely with MMB during late 2004 to prepare a budget that sought funds for an eighty-clinic project and also for sanitation projects, schools, and teacher housing. The anonymous donor's contact stayed abreast of changes and milestones through quarterly reports from Mano a Mano, frequent meetings with us, and trips to Bolivia to view the projects in person. Because of this ongoing flow of information, the anonymous donor did not request a formal second proposal. The budget was deemed appropriate and was approved.

Unlike the first grant, which was based solely on performance and documentation of expenditures, the payment terms for this second grant included matching requirements. The donor phased in the distribution of grant funds over a period of ten years and mandated that Mano a Mano meet all matching requirements by December 31, 2009.

### Performance and Matching Requirements for Second Anonymous Donor Grant

*Community Clinics*

Complete construction of 126 clinics, plus the distribution of medical supplies. Total new funding for this area: $2,820,000, with a $900,000 matching requirement.

*Schools, Housing for Teachers, and Sanitation Infrastructure*

Total new funding for this area: $700,000, with a $700,000 matching requirement.

*Economic Development*

Commitment for a new initiative that would require a new grant proposal of $100,000, with a $100,000 matching requirement.

The donor further required that all funds from both the grant award and the matching funds be sent to MMB with none retained for any U.S. expenses incurred for the medical distribution program, administrative oversight of the grant, or fundraising. Additionally, funds raised to support MMNM and MMAA programs could not be used to match this second grant. The U.S. board didn't question; we accepted the grant with these restrictions and focused on raising matching funds to capture the full grant award.

Three board members and two volunteers formed a fundraising committee and developed a set of talking points accompanied by a PowerPoint presentation to show potential donors. Preparing these materials helped the group hone their message. It soon proved so difficult to identify potential new donors, however, that efforts shifted to foundations and individuals who were already major donors. We prepared and submitted numerous proposals. Fortunately, our intense fundraising efforts paid dividends. During 2006, it became clear that Mano a Mano would be able to meet the matching fund requirements and the fundraising committee disbanded.

As with the anonymous donor's previous grant, we continued to prepare quarterly program performance reports and biannual reports on the matching funds we had raised. All funds from the matching donors and the anonymous donor were transferred to Bolivia to cover expenditures. All of the grant goals and requirements will have been met by 2014, when the anonymous donor's funding ends.

With the infusion of this sizable new grant and matching funds, Mano a Mano created an exemplary community clinic program in Bolivia. As a result, hundreds of thousands of rural residents' health and educational opportunities have improved.

## Supporting Mano a Mano in the United States

In our eagerness to obtain the anonymous donor's second grant in 2004, Mano a Mano's U.S. board members failed to recognize that its stringent demands and prohibition on using any portion of funds to cover costs in the United States would seriously limit the organization's capacity to function long term. At that point, the U.S. office had no paid staff. The intensive effort to raise matching funds depended almost entirely on Segundo and me. Concurrently, we continued to manage the volunteer program and all the day-to-day work of the organization.

In 2005, Segundo retired from Northwest Airlines. His retirement enabled him to devote eighty-hour weeks to Mano a Mano. Despite health limitations, I continued to write grant proposals and take primary responsibility for communications with donors, volunteers, and the public. We hired one staff person to assist with this workload.

In 2006, while strenuous efforts to fund clinic and education infrastructure projects continued, we also increased our efforts to raise funds to support the staggering U.S. workload. We gradually expanded the organization's mailing list, which resulted in a modest individual donation increase. In addition, we informed foundation officers of the need to fund the local operation. As a result of these efforts, one foundation that had funded several Mano a Mano projects in Bolivia awarded a multi-year grant to support Mano a Mano's U.S. office and volunteer program. By June, we had raised sufficient dollars to fund all U.S. budget items, including salaries for a director and two staff members, for the next eighteen months. With stringent oversight of expenses, Mano a Mano hired its first executive director in the United States that year.

At that point, the Mano a Mano board decided to expand its focus to include targeted fundraising for MMNM and MMAA by identifying donors with specific interests in water projects and aviation. These efforts resulted in new funding from donors who did not question Mano a Mano's inclusion of U.S. program expenses in proposed grant budgets.

## New Fundraising Strategies

At this stage Dan Narr, the new executive director, devoted most of his time to fundraising. He broadened Mano a Mano's strategies to pursue new resources, including businesses and corporate foundations. He began by searching for businesses that might donate to Mano a Mano. This extensive and time-consuming effort yielded several possibilities, including a pharmaceutical company interested in expanding into the Latin American market and a company that owns gold mines in Bolivia.

Pursuing business donations initially proved elusive. Businesses expect their philanthropic efforts to align with their business goals, and Bolivia is a very small market for an international company. Although several businesses showed interest, it was difficult to match their goals with Mano a Mano's needs and Bolivia's financial and political environment. Nevertheless, several local small business owners not so focused on their own business interests did contribute (based largely on Mano a Mano's stellar results). Over time, our persistence prevailed. A multinational corporation began to provide major funding for road and water projects. More recently, several Minnesota-based corporations have become engaged in local volunteer activities and have begun to provide some financial support through these relationships.

Dan's second strategy was to increase the number and size of individual donations. He reached out to churches and community groups, made presentations, encouraged interested persons to travel to Bolivia, and expanded the organization's mailing list. He spent countless hours responding to questions from interested individuals, updating them on Mano a Mano projects, and searching for new leads. The mailing list increased more than fourfold—from 1,325 people in 2006 to 5,854 in 2011.

Mano a Mano needed to expand its network of people interested in our work. One couple who had recently returned from a trip to Bolivia with Mano a Mano provided a great opportunity. They offered to sponsor a fundraising gala at their country club and invite their friends. Another recent traveler to Bolivia, a professional event planner, offered to plan the gala for a much-reduced fee. Mano a Mano volunteers formed a committee to plan the event. The gala planning group decided to feature Mano a Mano's clinic program with the objective that the gala might raise funds to build another rural clinic in Bolivia. At the event itself, Bolivian dancers and musicians welcomed and entertained the guests. Segundo and I talked briefly about why we created Mano a Mano and why we continue to devote our lives to its work. A live auction of donations added to the festivities and featured the weeklong use of a condo in Mexico, a Bolivian dinner with Segundo and me, a handmade quilt, Minnesota Twins tickets, and a few other items. Over 160 guests attended our first gala and collectively raised enough to build a clinic.

The second gala, held in 2011, followed a similar format and raised enough funds to build a small ravine water reservoir. In addition to raising funds at the event itself, the planning group hoped to draw new donors into the Mano a Mano fold and have a good time with current volunteers and donors. One guest announced at the end of evening, "I don't want the program to end yet. Last week I attended a gala for another organization. The program was so boring I just wanted to put my head down on the table and take a nap. Tonight I've had so much fun that I'm not ready to go home."

Despite Mano a Mano's increased efforts, since 2008 fundraising has been extremely challenging. Our repeated grant requests to already supportive donors left the organization vulnerable to the major economic downturn, when foundations and individuals saw their investments precipitously decline. At the same time, Mano a Mano reached the funding limits (maximum of three years for many) of several of its foundation supporters. As it became necessary to seek new funding sources, identifying potential donors became much more difficult.

With extreme frugality and the dependable dedication of our team in both the United States and Bolivia, Mano a Mano has continued to fund all of its programs. Our broadened donor base, with a stronger emphasis on individual and business donors, has helped make this possible.

While we have made significant progress in obtaining reliable funding to support the U.S. office, Mano a Mano continues to depend heavily on Segundo and me to assist with this work. Members of the board have long recognized that this arrangement is not indefinitely sustainable and are always considering ways to address this ongoing concern.

## Sources of Funding

The amount of funds raised between January 2005 and December 2010 far exceeded those raised in Phase III. During Phase IV, Mano a Mano received its first major gift from a corporate source, and other smaller businesses contributed funds to match the gift. The corporate donor has continued to support our road and water projects. Also, our concentrated effort to identify new individual prospects yielded a dramatic step up in individual giving. Increased funds from individuals, businesses, and foundations all made a measurable difference.

By the beginning of Phase IV, rural municipal officials and members of the communities they represent had become thoroughly familiar with the Mano a Mano partnership model. Their requests for assistance began to include a presentation of what each partner would contribute to the project. As Bolivia's national government has directed a gradually increasing proportion of the country's income toward projects in rural areas, municipalities have made larger contributions toward their projects. Currently, funds raised by Mano a Mano in the United States leverage contributions in Bolivia of up to fifty percent of a project's total cost.

# Lessons Learned in Phase IV

*Funding to support administration and fundraising activities is essential.* Although many donors chose to support Mano a Mano because of its very low administrative and fundraising expenses, an organization simply cannot sustain itself at a starvation level over the long term. As Mano a Mano's founders, we have devoted many years of our lives to the organization and its mission. The same is true for the Bolivian founders. It is unrealistic to expect that our eventual replacements will be willing or able to work at that pace without compensation. We have engaged in succession planning for several years, but our plans cannot be executed until funding can support them. To ensure the future health of the organization, administrative and fundraising personnel must be included in all annual budgets and funding requests. In retrospect, Mano a Mano should have appealed to the anonymous donor to reconsider his second grant's requirement that no funds could be used to cover the growing expenses of collecting and shipping supplies for the clinics or for managing and accounting for the grant. When Mano a Mano received the first anonymous donor grant for the clinic program, we were a small organization with modest accomplishments. That grant brought Mano a Mano more funds than we had raised in our first seven years combined. It never occurred to us to question any of its terms. However, by the time Mano a Mano received the second grant, we had demonstrated the capacity to surpass grant objectives, manage the funds, raise additional funding, and report to the donor. With our established track record, we should have requested funds to increase our administrative capacity and thus ensure a stable basis from which to sustain the community clinic program after the donor funds had been spent.

*Communicate regularly with individual donors.* Foundations usually require specific reports on the results of projects they've funded. Individual donors rarely do. Successful communication with individual donors depends on learning what motivates the donor, what has inspired the donor's interest in a specific type of project, and what type of communication the donor prefers. Mano a Mano tailors the frequency, medium, and content of our communications to individual donors. For example, some donors prefer to receive brief updates on the progress of their project of interest via e-mail. Others want a phone call that gives them an opportunity to ask questions and discuss any issues.

And still others respond best to sitting together and enjoying a meal as they learn more about the work of the organization. We spend a considerable amount of time speaking directly with individual donors. Relationships are essential to success.

*Keep volunteers and donors close to beneficiaries through travel opportunities.* The most exquisitely produced brochures, videos, and photos cannot convey the essence of the organization. Nothing provides the depth of a personal connection better than a visit to one of Mano a Mano's projects in Bolivia. One major donor, a social worker, visited a rural clinic and described its impact on her:

> *As we entered the clinic, its physician and nurse attended to a two-year old who had fallen and required stitches on her forehead. Several parents arrived to begin their class on healthy diets for young children. To our surprise, dozens of community residents who had seen our vehicle drive up to the clinic gathered in front of the building, greeted us enthusiastically, and told their stories of the difference Mano a Mano has made in their lives. Their young mothers had often died, they said, leaving orphaned children; now they come to the clinic to have their babies—and they live! The nurse teaches them about better diets and has helped them plant a vegetable garden in front of the clinic. They said the doctor is like a father to them. Recently, when a neighbor beat and severely injured his wife, they rushed the couple to the clinic. They said that the nurse could treat and comfort the wife, but the doctor must be the one to control the husband. They talked about the class the doctor is holding for men and said they are learning about how to respond to violence and alcoholism in their local families.*

*Hone the message.* Be clear about the need for a project, its goals, expected results, beneficiaries, and costs before approaching a donor. Most donors ask specific questions about details that are of particular interest to them. For example, large reservoir projects often stimulate questions about the heavy machinery. How is it moved from one location to another on treacherous mountain roads? What safety requirements do machine operators follow? What are the backgrounds of the engineers on staff? An organization that has looser ties with its distant ground operations might lack the on-the-spot answers to these questions. But Mano a Mano has found that our deep understanding of on-site detail assures donors that we are capable of managing and executing complex projects.

*Be prepared to present the next funding need.* At the conclusion of the Omereque water pond project, the staff arranged lunch with a donor couple to thank them for their donation and present project results. We did not intend to make another request over lunch but, when prompted, we knew our projects and needs well enough to present two options to them. We were relieved that they were enthusiastic about staying involved and continuing to contribute.

*Be flexible with funding sources.* Over the years, Mano a Mano has received funding from small family foundations, large corporate foundations, craft sales, individual donors, giving circles, events, and a substantial contribution from an anonymous donor. Many of these opportunities were serendipitous; many were the result of a lot of hard work eventually paying off. Comparison of our fundraising approach to many generally accepted best practices for fundraising would find us lacking. We would be considered overly reliant on a handful of foundations; we should focus on building up our individual donor base; and we should drop any fundraising events. While certain elements are definitely true (we are working hard to expand our individual donor base, for example), our approach has worked for us for almost twenty years, and we have made sure that we are in a position to take advantage of any opportunities as they arise. We never had any desire to do an annual fundraising event ourselves, but the opportunity presented itself and has been a successful project for years. Many foundations have gone way beyond their typical funding cycles and have been crucial to our success, even though that can make us overly reliant on their support. In short, we've found an approach that works for our unique situation.

*Require financial support from the community.* This point is vital; every project Mano a Mano takes on receives direct financial and in-kind support from the community and local municipal government. This is essential—to keep Mano a Mano's costs per project down and to ensure that the community has a stake in the project and will continue to stay involved. Our projects are built not just by Mano a Mano but by the communities themselves, and they take over ownership and administration of every project. We provide the seed money and skilled staff to make these projects a reality, but we are capitalizing on a huge level of commitment already present in each community.

◆ ◆ ◆ ◆

Mano a Mano has invested incalculable hours raising funds to help improve the health and economic well-being of poor Bolivians. Starting small and relying on in-kind donations meant that we needed minimal cash for the first few years of operation. As the organization grew, our funding needs increased as did our experience in how to identify, attract, and retain funders. The pool of funders broadened from a few individuals in Phase I with foundations added in Phase II and businesses in Phase IV. In addition to submitting tailored, well-researched grant proposals, we have tried a variety of other approaches aimed at relationship-building and connecting our donors to our on-the-ground activities in Bolivia. Visitors who see firsthand the impact of Mano a Mano's continuing work are often inspired to become part of it. As one prospective donor eloquently describes:

> *This organization has a unique understanding of and respect for the rural way of life and works with individual communities to meet specific needs. The great strength of Mano a Mano is that it is able to strike a balance between development and sustainability. Organizations with the vision, sensitivity, and capability of Mano a Mano are rare.*

# 10

# Organizational Design: Our Step-by-Step Evolution

*All organizations are perfectly designed to
get the results they get.*
—David P. Hanna, author of Designing Organizations
for High Performance[57]

It all began with a man and his suitcase. Mano a Mano's earliest program design was the essence of simplicity. As Segundo packed his suitcase in Mendota Heights, Minnesota, he left space for medical supplies that had been ready for the trash heap. On arrival in Cochabamba, Segundo delivered his medical stash to his brother José for use in a Bolivian hospital on the outskirts of town. That good deed, repeated over and over, accomplished its intended purpose and incidentally proved an elemental point: our great abundance might be shared. The result? Good feelings all around and the origin of an idea.

Segundo and I wanted to do more. In 1994, we incorporated

a low-budget, all-volunteer entity and applied for tax-exempt status as an IRS 501(c)(3) organization. Our early operations were narrow and focused. The name said it all. Mano a Mano Medical Resources collected surplus medical supplies and equipment in Minnesota and transported those items to Bolivia for the use of needy patients.

## Organizational Design at Start-Up

We started small. Mano a Mano's organizational framework was uncomplicated. There were nine members on that first board of directors. Founders (U.S. and Bolivian), officers, and board members contributed their time and expertise on a pro bono basis. Mano a Mano had no paid staff in the United States or Bolivia. The Bolivian founders worked with Bolivian volunteers to manage distribution of the medical supplies. Volunteers in the United States and in Bolivia ran the organization through an informal relationship-based structure. Minnesota volunteers, who numbered approximately thirty in 1994 and 200 by 1996, worked with an estimated fifty volunteers in Cochabamba. This simple structure and collegial atmosphere allowed the organization to self-correct quickly and with little effort.

During Phase I (1994–96), Mano a Mano had no physical assets. Not a desk, not a chair, not a computer. No cars, no trucks. It had no real estate. The organization operated in borrowed space. Its address was our home address. Our kitchen table was the site of meetings, phone calls, bookkeeping, and correspondence. Other business was conducted in our basement, garage, an unused barn on our property, and in our backyard. The organization was a conduit for donated medical surplus, which was stored in and around our home. The organization had an account at the local bank, where donor funds were temporarily deposited.

# Development of the Organization's Design: Bolivian Counterparts

Over the span of nineteen years, Mano a Mano grew from an organization that collected 500 pounds of medical supplies for a hospital in Bolivia to one that implemented successful infrastructure projects in eight of the country's nine departments (states). Expansion required changes in the organization's structure.

Mano a Mano's transformation was incremental. In 1994 and 1995, we collected and distributed surplus medical supplies. In 1996, we built satellite clinics in two barrios just outside Cochabamba. By 1997, we had determined to start building clinics in rural villages higher up in the Andes. These geographic and program expansions fell within Mano a Mano's start-up mission and required no structural changes.

Back in Minnesota, all was as it had been. As founders, we continued to absorb both the cost and effort required to oversee the medical supply distribution program in the United States. But in 1998 the board decided to fund two paid positions in Bolivia. The first was a part-time project director; the second, a full-time manager to handle the increasing volume of medical inventory. In addition, the board added a line item to clinic construction budgets to cover one or two master carpenters. These employees reported to a volunteer steering team in Bolivia composed of ten medical professionals. The relationship between the Bolivian steering team and the U.S. office, based on trust and frequent communication, remained informal.

## Creating the Legal Entity Mano a Mano Bolivia

As the amount of medical surplus continued to expand and the number of clinic projects grew, it became clear that a largely informal volunteer effort could not be expected to manage the increasing complexity in Bolivia. Near the end of Phase

II (1999), Mano a Mano's U.S. board encouraged the Bolivian steering team to collaborate on the creation of a legal entity in Bolivia.

The steering team members had two pressing concerns. First, they wanted a structure that prevented personnel shifts that might detrimentally affect the organization's mission. Second, they had to figure out how to comply with U.S. tax law yet establish an organization in which Bolivians retain control of daily operations while remaining accountable to the U.S. organization.

With these challenges at the forefront, steering team members in Bolivia, in consultation with the U.S. board, developed a governance structure and wrote bylaws. María Blanca Velásquez, a family member, contributed her legal expertise at no charge and completed the legal processes required to create a nonprofit organization under Bolivian law. The resulting documents formalized the relationship between this new organization and Mano a Mano in the United States.

The following article included in the Mano a Mano Bolivia bylaws addressed the intent to create the desired balance between the Bolivian and U.S. organizations:

> *Mano a Mano USA has the right to veto in Mano a Mano Bolivia aspects related to its own interests and in situations where the resolutions, agreements, work, results or other matters harm or are not in agreement with the objectives or philosophy of the organization (Chap 3, Art 19, e).*
>
> *Mano a Mano USA, in order to protect its interests, with support of 30 percent of Mano a Mano Bolivia is able to intervene in Mano a Mano Bolivia to restructure it…for reasons of loss of objectives, radical departure from the same, fraudulent use or misuse of funds, inadequate personnel or direction (Chap 3, Art 19, f).*

The Bolivian counterpart organization has full authority to respond to requests for assistance, design projects, establish work processes, and spend U.S.-raised funds—but they must do so in accordance with U.S. law, donor designations, and guidelines established by the Mano a Mano U.S. board.

The newly created organization chose the name Mano a Mano Bolivia (MMB) and became a recognized legal entity in Bolivia in 1999. Members formed an *asamblea*, in which they would all be permanent founding members as long as they continued to live in Bolivia. Named as a founder, Segundo was granted exemption from the Bolivian residency requirement. An *asamblea*, which oversees an organization's operations, is a common structural element in Bolivian nonprofits. From a sub-set of its members, the *asamblea* may create a board of directors to oversee the organization's day-to-day operations.

MMB was not created as a subsidiary of Mano a Mano U.S. It was instead incorporated as a Bolivian NGO under Bolivian law.

## MMB's Expanded Operations

During its start-up years (1999–2000), MMB administered the medical supplies program on the receiving end, supervised construction of two clinics per year, and made plans for the thirty-clinic program. During Phase III (2001–04), MMB came into full operation, funded primarily through the anonymous donor grant. It also completed the thirty-clinic project. Concurrently, MMB responded to requests from communities in the clinic network for sanitation infrastructure, school classrooms, and housing for teachers. Incidental to these projects, MMB improved arterial roads and aircraft landing strips near clinic communities. During this phase, MMB grew as a result of the plan set forth in the anonymous donor grant and budget, which included an executive director in Bolivia and manager positions relating to medical distribution, health care and health education, and construction. An accountant was also funded.

Each manager and the accountant had authority to make decisions during the MMB executive director's absence from the office. Consistent with plans and budgets, MMB put up an office building large enough to house its staff of twelve, built a warehouse to accommodate the increased quantity of medical supplies—200,000 pounds per year—and later purchased a lot for the vehicles and heavy equipment used to construct rural clinics and schools and support their operations.

## Creating Mano a Mano Apoyo Aéreo

During Phase IV (2005–Present), Mano a Mano initiated the creation of two new counterpart organizations in response to donor concerns.

In 2005, Mano a Mano created a second Bolivian counterpart organization, Mano a Mano Apoyo Aéreo (MMAA). The director of the donor foundation that funded equipment purchases required that the aviation program be incorporated as a Bolivian NGO separate from MMB. This donor stipulation was based on the foundation's extensive experience with aviation operations and conviction that: an aviation operation requires a board with aviation expertise, a business-minded aviation program might become self-supporting, and a separate entity protects counterpart entities' assets from liability claims. This second Bolivian counterpart organization was created to own and manage the aviation program.

The U.S. board agreed that these donor requirements were reasonable and supported the best interests of the entire Mano a Mano organization. Mano a Mano accepted the donation of the aviation program on this basis and proceeded to create the new organization. Initially, the MMB board expressed opposition, resisted the incorporation of a new organization, suggested that it assume control of the aviation program, and declined to appoint a representative to the aviation board. This difference in opinion delayed the incorporation process. Once MMAA was formed and operational, however, the two organizations worked together to achieve their mutual goals.

Program responsibilities for MMAA included emergency rescue, emergency food and supply airlifts in response to natural disasters, weekend clinics to serve tribal populations, staff visits to remote communities as distant as 475 miles from Cochabamba, and income-generating enterprises to make the organization self-supporting. In creating this new organization in Bolivia, the U.S. board chose a structure that did not include an *asamblea*. The board was convinced that this structural layer added unnecessary complexity to the inherent challenges of cross-national communication.

Drawing on his background in aviation and his familiarity with aviation-specific challenges and the intended role this organization would play in delivering rural health care, Segundo began to seek members for the new board. The board, as finally constituted, included a pilot with thirty years of experience flying in Bolivia, an attorney, an auditor, a banker, and a physician. The pilot chaired the board. Board members chose the name Mano a Mano Apoyo Aéreo (air support) for their new organization.

Segundo, as president of the U.S. board, became the official founder of MMAA. Its bylaws focused its board on the MMAA mission and program operations while protecting the interests of Mano a Mano U.S.

## Creating Mano a Mano Nuevo Mundo

During 2005, Mano a Mano also created a third Bolivian counterpart organization, Mano a Mano Nuevo Mundo (MMNM), to focus on economic development. This additional organization was created, in part, to limit liability and assist with funding.

Convinced by previous arguments our aviation donors made, Mano a Mano's board determined there were also grounds to limit liability potential relating to road construction. The board reasoned that similar liability concerns applied where heavy equipment and treacherous terrain were involved. Accordingly, the board formed a third organization to own and operate the heavy equipment required to complete road and water projects. Funding advantages were also an impetus. Some foundations and other funding entities outside of the United States are only interested in local Bolivian organizations, not those that are U.S.-based. The new organization also responded to donor scrutiny. In discussions of possible funding, USAID personnel raised serious concerns that road projects did not fit within a health organization—i.e., MMB—run by a physician.

The creation of MMNM provided organizational focus. Opting for a standalone organization instead of consolidation, the U.S. board made certain that road and water infrastructure projects received priority attention from experts. It also meant a flatter organizational structure by limiting the hierarchy that evolves out of the increased complexity when an organization adds programs. As the U.S. board resolved to increase organizational capacity in Bolivia, we determined that the creation of another well-run Bolivian nonprofit could involve more Bolivians in decision-making roles.

Segundo, as president of the U.S. board, became the official founder of this third counterpart organization and began seeking members to serve on its board. Board members included an accountant, an attorney, a construction business owner, and a carpentry business owner. The new board selected the name Mano a Mano Nuevo Mundo (MMNM) for their organization. MMNM's governing structure and bylaws closely resemble those of MMAA.

With input from its MMAA and MMNM counterparts, in 2005 the U.S. board prepared planning documents for use in guiding these organizations' development. Those initial planning documents are reviewed and updated regularly. From the outset, Mano a Mano U.S. has maintained frequent and regular contact with both organizations via Skype.

## Creating Mano a Mano Internacional

In 2012, Mano a Mano created a fourth Bolivian counterpart organization, Mano a Mano Internacional (MMI), to focus on fundraising, hosting foreign travelers and volunteers, piloting new projects, and training. We agreed at the outset that this organization would work more closely with Mano a Mano U.S. and would take responsibility for piloting new projects.

# Rationale for the Organizational Design of Mano a Mano's Bolivian Counterparts

Many U.S.-based organizations choose to form host country subsidiaries over which they exercise full control. In contrast to the organizational structure of many international nonprofits, the Mano a Mano board decided not to create satellite offices in Bolivia that would report to a large core office staff in the United States. Instead, in accordance with the philosophy and practice that has been the hallmark of Mano a Mano, the U.S. board insisted on local control. We helped interested, capable, and trustworthy Bolivians create legal, fully-formed Bolivian nonprofit organizations to function as counterparts to Mano a Mano U.S. We focused on building organizational capacity that advances Mano a Mano's mission in Bolivia. We see the following advantages in adopting this structure:

- **Formalizes the successful bottom-up model** that Mano a Mano developed through the distribution of medical surplus and the early community clinic program.

- **Expands capacity in Bolivia.**

- **Recognizes that Bolivians are the experts** on programs in Bolivia and relies on Bolivian personnel to actively shape programs, attain an understanding of a community's needs, assess the community's commitment level, note the reputation and interest of local leaders, ascertain the availability of local funding support, and consider the laws and customs that provide the context in which projects will be undertaken.

- **Expedites projects.** The Bolivian organizations select communities in which to work, determine the project size and design, and proceed with implementation—consistent with program goals and prior planning with the U.S. office.

- **Positions organizations to apply for funds** that directly benefit in-country NGOs, such as businesses that extract natural resources from Bolivia and choose to fund programs that improve the well-being of residents in surrounding communities; modest-sized, Bolivian-owned businesses that award grants for water projects when a Bolivian NGO is involved; other countries, including Canada, most EU countries, and Japan, who provide modest funding to Bolivian NGOs through their embassies.

- **Connects our counterpart organizations to the mission established by the Mano a Mano U.S. board,** mitigates the fear that future members of the *asamblea* or board could divert Mano a Mano funds, and thwarts any possible misuse of funds by retaining legal control in the hands of founders in the United States and in Bolivia.

- **Establishes clear accountability for funds transferred to Bolivia from the United States** through internal and external (IRS, state) oversight.

- **Minimizes the likelihood that differences between the Bolivian and U.S. governments** will
lead to reprisals against Mano a Mano programs.
Being fully registered as a nonprofit in Bolivia allows Mano a Mano to avoid, or at least minimize,
tensions that can arise politically and affect U.S.-
based organizations.

Mano a Mano's bilateral structure does have drawbacks. The give-and-take inherent in such a structure encourages a con-sensus-based approach to decision-making on major issues. Conversations must usually be translated, which takes time, so lengthy conversations sometimes create frustration. For this rea-son, many NGOs and other organizations conclude that making decisions from a central U.S. office and requiring that they be implemented in the field is easier and less frustrating. Howev-er, Mano a Mano's experience has affirmed our long-standing belief that the time and effort spent on consensus-building pays dividends many times over.

## Tax Implications of Our Organizational Design

The above-described structure has expanded our organizational capacity in Bolivia. At the same time, it has ensured account-ability by: including representatives of the U.S. board on the Bolivian governing bodies, giving veto authority to the U.S. or-ganization, and transferring funds on a reimbursement basis. Most U.S. donors deem 501(c)(3) status essential when deciding whether and how much to contribute to a nonprofit. To main-tain its nonprofit status, Mano a Mano must be a good steward of others' generous donations by meeting all IRS requirements. For a donation to a 501(c)(3) organization that completes projects in a foreign country to be classified as a charitable deduction, the U.S. organization must have legal controls over the foreign organization; review and approve the projects for which funds will be spent; monitor and oversee the foreign project through field review; retain full control of donated funds; and exercise discretion as to their use, even to the point of retaining the right to terminate further funding and withdraw unspent funds at any time. In view of these requirements, Mano a Mano U.S. has guaranteed that it will always have representation and veto authority over its four Bolivian counterparts.

Gifts to nonprofits do not yield tax-related benefits for donors in Bolivia because there is no comparable tax code, nor are Bolivian nonprofit organizations exempt from sales or property taxes. Bolivian organizations incorporate as *sin fines de lucro* (without goals of profit-making), entities that must apply all organizational assets and earnings to their humanitarian or social service mission. Under Bolivian law, no individual or entity may benefit by taking profit from organizations registered in this way.

Bolivian nonprofits may enjoy the advantage of duty-free status for items received from outside the country, a significant financial advantage. While Mano a Mano did not have its own duty-free agreement with the Bolivian government, all of its medical cargo entered Bolivia on a duty-free basis through Catholic Relief Service (CRS) and its duty-free agreement through 2010. When revised customs-related laws made it impossible for CRS to continue to provide this benefit for Mano a Mano, the CRS attorney in Bolivia enlisted the aid of a customs attorney in the capital city of La Paz, who was successful in obtaining permission for Mano a Mano cargo to continue to enter the country without paying duty.

In some instances, Mano a Mano has elected to pay customs duty. Any item that a nonprofit brings into Bolivia on a duty-free basis must be used to either fulfill the organization's mission or be sold or donated to another nonprofit organization. When importing aircraft and heavy machinery, Mano a

Mano has elected to remain flexible by paying customs duty. It has thus retained the ability to sell imported equipment on the open market and then purchase new or more useful equipment needed to complete projects.

## Changes in Mano a Mano's Structure

From its inception in 1994, Mano a Mano and its U.S. board created the organizational vision, raised funds, planned and co-ordinated programs, exercised financial oversight, operated the U.S. medical surplus program, and focused on results and sus-tainability. Over the years, our primary adaptations involved the creation of four counterpart organizations in Bolivia.

### Revision of Mission for Mano a Mano U.S.

Given our decision to extend programs in Bolivia to include infrastructure for sanitation and education for communities within the clinic network, the U.S. board voted in May 2001 to update Mano a Mano's articles of incorporation to reflect this expansion.

Mano a Mano's original mission statement, created in 1994, stated: "To increase the capacity of health-care providers in Bo-livia to serve impoverished patients." It focused on cooperative efforts to address Bolivian health-care needs, but did not ac-count for the creation of separate legal entities in Bolivia.

Not surprisingly, Mano a Mano's successful implementation of the community-driven clinic program inspired community requests for related projects that indirectly supported our orig-inal vision. These requests involved schools that taught health education along with reading and writing, roads connecting communities, and sanitation infrastructure.

In December 2004, the board expanded the organization's vision to reflect more explicitly the education and infrastructure components that contribute significantly to our stated health objectives. The expanded vision statement positioned the organization to afford recognition to the growth of community requests for water and road projects and to frame funding appeals to address these projects: "To improve the health and extend the life span of impoverished Bolivians by increasing the capacity of health-care providers and communities to address their medical, community development, and educational needs."

In 2005, Mano a Mano's U.S. board updated and reworded our mission statement again, this time to embrace the organization's emphasis on partnerships and reflect its expanded work in economic development. The revised language explicitly acknowledged the notion that Mano a Mano would work in partnership with rural Bolivian villages to accomplish our purpose. Here is the mission statement currently in effect: "To create partnerships with impoverished Bolivian communities to improve health and increase economic well-being."

### Revision of Legal Name for Mano a Mano U.S.

In 2008, Mano a Mano's board of directors took a big step in the right direction. We changed the organization's name from Mano a Mano Medical Resources, a name we had clearly outgrown, to Mano a Mano International Partners.

## Mano a Mano's Current Organizational Design

Twenty years after its creation, Mano a Mano's work in the United States continues much as before. Mano a Mano now has office space and a warehouse. Dedicated desks have replaced our kitchen table. But the work on the ground is much the same. Weekends still find Minnesota volunteers sorting and packing.

Mano a Mano International Partners—also routinely referred to as just Mano a Mano and as Mano a Mano U.S.—carries out its responsibilities as described in the preceding chapters. In summary, Mano a Mano U.S.:

**1. Develops the organizational vision and mission.**

**2. Creates and takes responsibility for the organization's overall structure.**

In keeping with our primary role, Mano a Mano has crafted an organizational structure designed to give maximum autonomy to Bolivian boards and staff while ensuring that the U.S. office retains control of the receipt and expenditure of funds donated by U.S. residents and organizations. With attention to sustainable growth that assures innovation, supports organizational goals, and brings needed resources to core programs, Mano a Mano U.S. adheres to these principles:

- Expand programs and create counterpart organizational structures through an intentional process that takes into consideration organizational capacity, budgetary implications, and feasibility of success.

- Expand into new program areas with implications for our counterpart organizations in Bolivia only after ensuring that the new program: fits with our mission, values, vision, and model; fits with our organizational capabilities; is likely to be successful; will meet a need that has been identified at the community level; has potential to bring resources into current programs; and presents opportunities for beneficial partnerships.

**3. Raises funds.**

To fulfill our mission, Mano a Mano U.S. solicits funds to support our programs and manages relationships with all potential and current donors. Mano a Mano U.S. does not outsource fundraising. Instead, we research worldwide databases for foundation-, government-, and organization-based grant opportunities. We seek opportunities to present Mano a Mano to churches, civic organizations, and individuals and then prepare and present written communication, in-person presentations, proposals, and other materials, as appropriate to the funding source. We prepare project budgets and ensure that any funding we receive is restricted according to the donor's wishes. We inform the appropriate Mano a Mano organization in Bolivia of the gift. We prepare interim and final reports of accomplishments and expenditures for the donor.

Mano a Mano U.S. exercises full discretion and control of all funds received for Mano a Mano projects, as required by the IRS, through strict adherence to these protocols:

- Review, approve, and authorize the project design and the method through which it will be implemented—all prior to soliciting funds.

- Exercise control of project implementation and expenditure of funds by retaining the right to veto any decision made by the Mano a Mano organizations in Bolivia in relation to projects funded by Mano a Mano U.S.

- Monitor project implementation and expenditure of funds through reports submitted to Mano a Mano U.S. by the Mano a Mano organizations in Bolivia.

- Conduct site visits.

- Retain control of grant-sourced funds through our budgeting process.

- Ensure that funds are used to carry out the mission of Mano a Mano U.S. by retaining the right to terminate further funding, as well as withdraw unspent funds, if it determines that funds have been used in a manner that is incompatible with the mission of Mano a Mano U.S. or for an unapproved purpose.

- Share this policy with donors for projects that are implemented or operated by Mano a Mano organizations in Bolivia.

**4. Assures compliance with all legal requirements governing not-for-profits and assumes responsibility for fiscal management.**

From the outset, Mano a Mano U.S. has paid special attention to IRS requirements for tax-exempt international organizations and also to Minnesota state requirements. In timely compliance with the federal and state requirements, we keep careful records of income and expenditures and require our counterpart organizations in Bolivia to submit receipts for expenditures. We track the receipt and disposition of all in-kind items for report to regulatory authorities. All fund transfers require two signatures from preauthorized board members or the executive director. We hire independent auditors, given that the organization has passed the federal income threshold ($350,000) and the state threshold ($25,000). We also file the required yearly statements of financial support with the Minnesota attorney general's office and the IRS.

**5. Communicates with interested parties and entities.**

Through our staff and governing board, Mano a Mano U.S. develops and manages methods for communicating about Mano a Mano with regulatory entities, donors, volunteers, other organizations and institutions, and the general public. All communication, whether its audience is internal or external, is based on and reflects the organization's commitment to accountability, good stewardship, transparency, accuracy, sustainability, and respect for the communities in which its projects are completed. To ensure that all potential and actual donors receive accurate, consistent, and compelling messages that relate to their interests and concerns, Mano a Mano U.S. assumes responsibility for all communication with them.

**6. Manages a medical surplus collection program.**

To increase the capacity of Bolivian health-care providers to serve their impoverished patients, Mano a Mano U.S. remains responsible for identifying medical care providers and vendors in the United States that have surplus medical supplies, equipment, and related items. We seek donations of these items and arrange their transport to Bolivia for use in facilities constructed by Mano a Mano and other programs that serve the poor. We require regular reports from Bolivia in regard to the distribution of medical cargo.

**7. Oversees a volunteer program.**

Mano a Mano U.S. accomplishes our work primarily through a cadre of talented and committed volunteers. We recruit, train, schedule, assign work, and recognize volunteers; they are a mainstay of the organization. We are committed to: treating volunteers with respect, assigning work that is meaningful to them, honoring their time limitations, and nurturing their relationship with the organization.

**8. Plans trips to Bolivia.**

The Mano a Mano U.S. organization plans trips to Bolivia for potential and current donors, volunteers, and other interested persons. These highly customized trips have two goals: to provide an opportunity for travelers to see Mano a Mano projects firsthand, and to develop a committed cadre of passionate advocates who will return to the United States and tell the Mano a Mano story.

## 9. Engages in research and education.

Several institutions of higher education have expressed interest in collaborating with Mano a Mano U.S. in the joint development of research and educational programs that will contribute to both partners' ability to fulfill our respective missions. To this end, Mano a Mano U.S. co-teaches formal classes and co-directs student research and evaluation projects that are feasible and relevant to both entities. Experiences are designed to meet the requirements of each institution and its respective programs. To further develop our potential to add to the body of knowledge on how to effect positive change at the community level in developing countries and attract major potential donors, Mano a Mano U.S. explores and responds to opportunities to publish our research information through juried journal articles and other media. Going forward, Mano a Mano U.S. intends to increase our formative evaluation and field research capacity.

## 10. Assures accountability, transparency, frugality, and freedom from corruption.

At the outset, we took all sensible steps to earn a reputation for integrity in the United States and Bolivia. Mano a Mano U.S. instituted systems to ensure transparency and accountability. Over the years, Mano a Mano developed and adhered to various measures to guarantee verifiable integrity in its operations.

We use a detailed and highly transparent inventory system to track every item shipped in connection with the surplus medical supply program. A bar-code system facilitates tracking in-kind donations and improves our efficiency. We set up a number of internal protocols to avoid any suspicion of official or volunteer theft. For example, detailed lists of every item boxed for shipment are made; boxes are presented to health-facilities officials along with recorded lists of their contents; boxes are unpacked in front of officials with additional staff members present; and lists of shipments' contents are posted on the wall for all to review.

By design, we rely on the energy and expertise of volunteers at all levels of the organization to the safest and most expedient extent possible. Another aspect of our frugality and careful stewardship of precious resources is figuring the exact quantity of building materials (e.g., by counting bricks) to be transported to a clinic, school, or infrastructure project site in order to avoid waste.

Mano a Mano is resolved to resist any bribery attempts in Bolivia and insistent on strict adherence to this principle at every level of the organization.

## Mano a Mano's Bolivian Counterparts

Each Bolivian counterpart organization is responsible for planning and implementing a portion of Mano a Mano's overall mission. Mano a Mano U.S. has near-daily contact with each of our Bolivian counterparts.

Each of Mano a Mano's Bolivian counterpart organizations is a distinct legal entity, incorporated through the governor's office in the department (state) of Cochabamba. They have no legal connection to each other as Bolivian entities. Funds and assets are not jointly owned or comingled. The policy and program decisions of each are made independently, though their actions are often coordinated to advance their shared Mano a Mano mission.

Relationships among the Mano a Mano organizations in Bolivia are informal and personal, not codified through bylaws or formal agreements. For example, MMAA provides air transport for staff of MMB and MMNM to distant sites to initiate and supervise projects, and also flies in urgently needed equipment and parts where necessary to prevent project delays. It flies MMB's volunteer medical professionals into remote areas of Bolivia to staff weekend clinics and responds to emergency requests for air rescue called in by MMB and MMNM. The three organizations' overarching missions and visions and clearly defined roles and responsibilities are central to their successful collaboration.

Organizational structures are relatively flat. Each counterpart has a board of directors. In the case of MMB, the board of directors is a subset of a larger *asamblea*. Each counterpart has bylaws approved by the department in which it resides. Each has a director, staff, and volunteers as needed to carry out its mission. Each is self-governing and operates as an independent entity in Bolivia. The U.S. board president plus two additional persons selected by the U.S. board serve on each counterpart's governing body and represent the interests of Mano a Mano U.S. These U.S. representatives have the authority to veto any resolution that would result in use of funds in a manner: inconsistent with the organization's vision, mission, or philosophy; inconsistent with the donor's wishes; or potentially harmful to the organization and the Mano a Mano mission. In case of extreme malfeasance, the U.S. board can take direct control of and restructure a counterpart organization.

## Lessons Learned about Organizational Design

*Follow a deliberate, considered process when expanding the mission.*

*Design the organization to deliver the mission.* As the mission expanded, Mano a Mano deliberately and thoughtfully reframed and expanded its structure to deliver new programs.

*Draw from the organization's values and philosophy to establish a context for organizational design.* Mano a Mano's capacity-building focus led to the adoption of its current design rather than the more typical organizational structure with a core office in the United States and an in-country satellite office.

*Form counterpart organizations that balance requirements for control of funds with strategies to build in-country leadership capacity.* The Bolivian counterpart organizations have authority to respond to requests for assistance, design their projects, establish their own work processes, and spend funds raised in the United States—so long as those expenditures are in accordance with U.S. law, donor designations, and guidelines established by the U.S. board.

*Establish separate legal entities for disparate work.* Having separate organizations assures organizational focus. It also limits liability and hierarchy, allowing a flatter structure that keeps staff in close contact with the rural community members who benefit from our projects.

*Define roles and responsibilities clearly.* Clarity of roles, responsibilities, and missions for Mano a Mano U.S. and counterpart organizations is crucial to assure smooth operations and minimize misunderstandings.

*Position the organization to meet newly defined needs and take advantage of new opportunities through flexible planning.* Mano a Mano U.S. develops three- to five-year plans to guide the organization's development and identify areas of interest if funding becomes available. However, actual project selection remains driven from the ground up, and the board remains flexible to respond to new needs and funding opportunities.

◆ ◆ ◆ ◆

Mano a Mano's organizational design and development evolved as the organization and mission grew. What started with an informal, relationship-based volunteer structure grew to a structure composed of Mano a Mano in the United States and four Bolivian counterpart nonprofits that provide employment for over 600 people, all but three of whom are in Bolivia. The structure was intentionally designed to support the organization's community-driven philosophy and our desire to keep staff close to the beneficiaries.

# 11

# The Mano a Mano Approach: Measuring Success

*By far the best proof is experience.*
—Sir Francis Bacon, philosopher and
creator of the scientific method

*Not everything that counts can be counted,*
*and not everything that can be counted counts.*
—William Bruce Cameron, sociologist

Mano a Mano's community-based approach delivers results. Perhaps the surest sign of Mano a Mano's success
is the community response. Seventeen years ago, Bolivian villagers were skeptical. We still recall the villager who called us
*ch'amas* (noisemakers who promise everything but do nothing).
On behalf of his community, he expressed doubt that Mano a
Mano would follow through on its plans and make it all work.
But in the case of that project, and the rest, Mano a Mano made

good on its word. Out there in the Andes, somehow the word spread. As rural Bolivian villages learned about Mano a Mano and the clinics and schools that had brought improved health care and educational options to distant communities, they clamored for the same attention. Our backlog of community requests for projects, which now number over 300, attests to Mano a Mano's successes.

While the best measurement may be the resounding reaction of Bolivian communities, Mano a Mano recognizes the need to evaluate ourselves with a more systematic approach. A paper trail has always seemed a sensible way to do that. From the beginning we have carefully tracked input, output, outcomes, and the many mundane details essential to make it all work.

## Evaluation and Data-Driven Decision-Making

Mano a Mano's approach to decision-making is data driven. Consistent review of information informs all organizational decisions. Our reliance on research, evaluation, and data-driven decision-making reflects our prior experience in the public and private sectors and draws on the writings of Michael Q. Patton and his development of the Utilization-Based Model in the manner described below.[58]

During its first few months of operation, Mano a Mano identified the decision-makers and stakeholders who would be the primary users of any information gathered. The next step was to define what questions the stakeholders and decision-makers hoped to answer and identify the purpose for which the information would be used. Finally, Mano a Mano created a framework and process for collecting needed information and ensured that it would be available to those making decisions regarding the organization's operations and programs. As we added new programs, we reviewed changing information needs in concert with Bolivian counterparts. Together, Mano a Mano U.S. and its Bolivian counterparts expanded data collection accordingly. The information collected included input (e.g., volunteer hours), output (e.g., number of clinics built), and outcomes (e.g., decreased mortality rates and increased income).

Mano a Mano identified five stakeholders as primary users of its information: our organization's boards, staff, volunteers, donors, and agencies with oversight responsibility in both Bolivia and the United States. Internal stakeholders are the most frequent users of the information collected. Initially, members of the U.S. board comprised this group. As the organization grew, the group expanded to include managers, staff members, and volunteers of each Mano a Mano organization.

## Input Data

From the start, Mano a Mano collected data on inputs. An almost daily task, then and now, is the review of input information for the medical surplus operation. Input data includes volunteer hours contributed, revenues collected, and types and weights of medical supplies and equipment obtained. This information is routinely shared and reviewed at board meetings.

At first, we recorded the information using simple manual forms and processes and used it to shape and form our actions. For example, after noting that the organization had developed good sources for handheld medical instruments but not for equipment like hospital beds, we began to contact nursing homes and subsequently received hundreds of donated beds. This simple example demonstrates the process and the immediate utility and impact of the data that is collected.

**Mano a Mano's Data Process**

**1. Identify decision-makers and stakeholders**

**needing information; what questions they hope**

**to answer; and the purpose of the information.**

**2. Create a framework and process for collecting data.**

**3. Have decision-makers regularly review the collected data.**

**4. Use the insights to make data-based decisions on programs and operations.**

## Output Data

Mano a Mano has also collected information on output from our earliest days. Initial output figures included pounds of medical inventory shipped to Bolivia and numbers of health-care facilities that received these medical donations. Creation of the clinic program required the tracking of items relating to clinic construction and operation. This data included numbers of clinics, and cost information. In preparing for its first major expansion of the clinic program, Mano a Mano developed an extensive set of forms for recording data on the requesting community and patient contact information.

Every time Mano a Mano added a new program, we developed forms for recording input and output information and a process for internal review. The staff in Bolivia uses the collected information to make management decisions. With the output data in hand, they schedule project tasks and determine whether requests for new projects can be accepted. Staff in the United States review the information quarterly and present it to the board of directors. In addition to identifying issues for discussion with counterpart staff in Bolivia, Mano a Mano uses input and output information virtually every day in conversations with our donors.

On several occasions in the past, volunteers have completed brief informal interviews with residents to gather their views on whether and how a project has made a difference in their communities. Through the collection of these kinds of qualitative, experiential responses from community residents, Mano a Mano has strengthened its information base. This type of data collection remains an ongoing process.

During the summer of 2011, a group of three graduate students in the field of international development completed interviews for Mano a Mano. The interviews, which required fluency in Spanish, were conducted in two rural Bolivian communities. The students went first to Omereque, where a water project had recently been completed. The second set of interviews was conducted in Sancayani, where a water project would be completed by year's end. Mano a Mano shared the findings internally and with residents of the two communities. The results were then used to shape later projects and will be used to shape future projects to help residents obtain maximum benefit from their water reservoir projects.

## Requests for Input and Output Data

There are two main external information users—donors and oversight organizations. Donors make up the larger contingent, though information requests and feedback may be informal. Oversight organizations often require formal reports.

Many donors are individuals who have heard about the organization from our board members, staff, volunteers, or website. These donors respond enthusiastically to input and output information and to the organization's many human interest stories.

Foundations, on the other hand, pose specific questions to which the organization must respond. These inquiries frequently come after the grant period ends. Foundations nearly always ask about the extent to which the organization accomplished the objectives listed in its grant proposal.

Foundations rarely request information about outcomes. Grant objectives generally focus on input and output, such as whether a partnership agreement had been completed and signed, a clinic built, and staff hired. Examples of other types of questions include: What will change in your organization as a result of this project? What barriers did you encounter? What did you learn? What other funds did you leverage? The responses to these questions emerge from discussions among staff about the specific project funded. Foundation staff review the reports submitted and take them into consideration when reviewing another funding request. Attesting to their satisfaction with our reported results, almost every foundation that has granted funds to Mano a Mano has awarded us more than one grant.

Other recipients of our collected input and output data include agencies with oversight responsibility in Bolivia and the United States. In order for Mano a Mano's Bolivian counterpart organizations to continue to operate, they must respond to questions from Bolivian agencies with oversight responsibility. The requested information typically includes both input and output data relating to personnel and the receipt and expenditure of funds. Additionally, the Ministry of Health requires extensive health-service data from the clinics.

In the United States, the IRS, the Minnesota attorney general's office, and the Charities Review Council request periodic reports. Much of the data required relates to the organization's finances and internal processes. Collection of this information makes it possible for the oversight body to evaluate whether the organization is fiscally sound and transparent. Failure to meet their reporting requirements could result in penalties to the organization and loss of donors and would seriously compromise its 501(c)(3) status.

## Outcome Data

As used by NGOs, the word *outcome* describes the statistical impact of charitable initiatives. Statistical analysis can be used to show a project's impact on mortality, literacy, or other "outcomes." Randomized evaluations have been used by larger charities and the microfinance industry to determine the impact of their programs. But these evaluation methods, which employ a control group, are costly and difficult to apply in a field, as opposed to laboratory, setting.

Mano a Mano has not, to date, collected extensive data on outcomes. Currently, our only systematically collected outcome information relates to maternal and infant mortality. We track the numbers of deliveries attended by Mano a Mano clinic staff members and the childbirth survival rates for mothers and infants.

While municipal agronomists tell Mano a Mano that the incomes of subsistence farm families double and triple once they receive water from the reservoir for their crops, we want to carefully document this important outcome through in-person interviews with the families. Additionally, in the future we hope to collect production, diet, and income data prior to initiating a project and again at two-year intervals for up to six years after a project is completed. In this way, we hope to obtain a clear picture of inputs that are required to ensure success. Mano a Mano expects to conduct similar interviews in communities in which we have built roads.

Mano a Mano has otherwise relied primarily on site visits, frequent in-person contact with beneficiaries, and systematic review of numbers and reports as evidence to assess the impact of our programs. This is, we have concluded, a reasonable approach for now. In the exercise of common-sense frugality, Mano a Mano has stuck with principles that have served us well: good medical care requires basic supplies; clinics, schools, water reservoirs, and roads matter for rural communities. As a long-term practice, Mano a Mano resolutely directs our available funds toward building and sustaining health care, education, and economic development infrastructure in Bolivia.

The output and outcome indicators Mano a Mano presents most often to donors and the general public include, as of April 2014:

- Shipped over 3.5 million pounds of usable medical surplus from Minnesota to Bolivia.

- Constructed and brought into full operation 145 community health clinics.

- For births attended by Mano a Mano doctors or nurses, the maternal mortality rate is 91 percent lower when compared to the available maternal mortality data for rural Bolivia.

- For births attended by Mano a Mano doctors or nurses, the infant mortality rate is 92.5 percent lower when compared to the available infant mortality data for rural Bolivia.

- Completed education infrastructure projects in forty-nine communities.

- Air lifted more than 2,166 patients to emergency care.

- Constructed or improved more than 1,400 kilometers (875 miles) of arterial rural roads, which can reduce travel time from days to hours.

- Doubled subsistence farm income, according to agronomists, through water projects that serve 30,000 people.

- All projects undertaken have been completed and continue to function.

## Difficult Challenges Faced

Mano a Mano's achieved results have far exceeded our initial vision for the organization, but our successes did not come easily. We encountered difficult challenges and obstacles along the way.

### The Cross-National, Cross-Cultural Nature of the Organization

Mano a Mano was the outgrowth of a deep connection with community, and it grew organically in response to needs articulated by those who would benefit from its programs. To address each identified problem, Mano a Mano has woven together the richness of knowledge, perspective, and practice that evolves from bicultural experience. As founders, we think of this as one of the organization's greatest assets. We sometimes reflect on those small stories that embody the innovations and inspirations that shape our evolving work in Bolivia.

When Segundo visited the building site of Clínica Gloria I, Mano a Mano's first clinic, he noted that thick, high-quality plastic sheeting had been placed between the foundation and the brick wall to keep it from absorbing salt from the soil. He asked the carpenter where he had found this type of plastic in Bolivia. "You sent it to us," the carpenter replied. Not recalling this item from the inventory, Segundo asked again and learned that the U.S. Air Force Reservists had used this plastic to cover the pallets of medical supply boxes en route to Bolivia. While we in the United States tend to think of tools and materials in relation to their intended purpose, our counterparts examine the article first, and then find a use for it. We have seen excess drain suction tubing used to strap down cargo on an SUV making its way to a project site or to repair a fuel line when the nearest repair shop is hours away. The bicultural founders could look at each potential gift from the United States and every need articulated in rural Bolivia and combine them in countless ways. This combination of expertise, resourcefulness, and need to "make do" with whatever the environment offered is at the core of Mano a Mano's success.

National and cultural differences have also led to difficulties, however—from misunderstandings later resolved through open discussions to those that continue to create tension. One example of an easily resolvable issue arose after Mano a Mano initiated travel experiences to Bolivia for its volunteers and donors. After a group of travelers returned home to Minnesota, one of Mano a Mano's Bolivian volunteers contacted the U.S. office to ask why it had sent someone to spy on them. She said everyone there was "up in arms" and making references to the CIA. After several minutes of discussion with us, the Bolivian volunteer understood that the traveler asked questions about the work because she was friendly and interested. The volunteer offered to share that explanation with others in Bolivia.

As a result of this concern, we routinely talk with travelers from the United States about how their Bolivian counterparts might perceive their direct questions. The U.S. volunteer came to recognize the importance of being more clear about why she asked questions and about providing similar types of information about activities in the U.S. office. This issue has not resurfaced but could have sparked years-long underlying tension if perspectives had not been shared.

The most difficult conflicts have arisen around the concept of respect. The sense that one is respected and respects others is integral to Latino culture. However, the U.S. perspective on what the Latino culture defines as respect is not respect, but deference. The Bolivian view of respect relates to lines of authority and one's position in relation to another. That hierarchical definition of respect, combined with Bolivia's history of having its resources exploited by developed countries and multinational corporations, can easily result in unwittingly triggering a Bolivian's sensitivity to being disrespected.

Tension arises when requirements that Mano a Mano must meet in the United States are perceived as disrespectful and interfering with the operational autonomy of our Bolivian counterpart NGOs. The issue becomes most difficult when it relates to a U.S. donor's specific requirements. Most foundations and many individuals fund only organizations that have a 501(c)(3) status. An organization that works internationally cannot function simply as a pass-through of funds if it is to maintain this status; it must approve all programs that receive its funding and retain control over expenditures, ensuring that they meet the requirements of the donor. Tensions surface periodically regarding some of these requirements. For example, donors expect the U.S. office to ultimately be responsible for managing their contributions, overseeing the projects they fund, and issuing the appropriate tax-exempt documentation. If a Bolivian counterpart circumvents the U.S. office and communicates directly with the donor, implying that its independent funding appeals are under the auspices of the U.S. office, it seriously jeopardizes the organization's ability to properly exercise its legal fiduciary responsibility. Managing this issue has been one of Mano a Mano's greatest challenges.

At times, the lack of full diplomatic relations between the United States and Bolivia has become a serious cross-national issue. The Bolivian government has taken steps to show opposition toward U.S. government policies. Effective December 1, 2007, U.S. citizens entering Bolivia as tourists were required to obtain a U.S. tourist visa. To enter the United States, Bolivian citizens must do the same. For Bolivians to obtain a U.S. tourist visa, they must complete a lengthy application, file numerous documents, and complete at least one in-person interview at the U.S. embassy in La Paz. Mano a Mano regularly wishes to bring staff, volunteers, and beneficiaries to the United States to meet with funders and participate in activities with volunteers. However, obtaining a visa for individuals with very low incomes or lack of property, especially rural project beneficiaries, has become nearly impossible.

Recently, the Bolivian government expelled the U.S. Agency for International Development (USAID) from the country. As a result, Mano a Mano is no longer eligible to ship cargo to Bolivia though USAID programs, a serious challenge as these programs allowed us to ship millions of pounds of donated cargo to Bolivia nearly for free; we now have to fundraise for each container we send.

## Lack of Infrastructure in Bolivia

Bolivia's lack of transportation infrastructure—roads, railways, airstrips, boats, or barges—creates daily obstacles for Mano a Mano staff and volunteers. Determined to serve neglected rural areas, these dedicated individuals spend untold hours driving on dangerous roads to reach communities that request our help. MMB's heartfelt thanks for funds to purchase new vehicles illustrates the extent of these daily challenges. Mano a Mano's initial response to a project request involves visiting the community, discussing the partnership model, and viewing the potential site. Lack of infrastructure magnifies the difficulties involved in arranging these meetings. Mano a Mano staff shared the following account of making a community visit:

> When the village of El Palmar presented its forty-nine-kilometer (thirty-mile) road project request, we made plans to fly to this distant region. When we arrived and met the El Palmar delegation, we learned that the mayor and several councilmen had traveled for two and a half days in order to reach the airstrip on time for this meeting, traveling the last half of the trip on horseback. The villagers had hoped that Mano a Mano

*could make a decision about the project after traveling a short distance into the area, but we knew that we must visually inspect the whole proposed route before making a commitment to build a mountain road. We promised to return with the intent of spending several days walking the entire forty-nine-kilometer distance, crossing mountains, valleys, and rivers on horseback to reach the gravel road at the other end. From there we would catch a bus to the nearest town where the Mano a Mano aircraft could pick us up and fly us to Cochabamba. Our full inspection convinced us that Mano a Mano could undertake this large and difficult project.*

Excerpt from an MMB staffer's note of thanks following the purchase of new vehicles:

*Staff has been very busy completing and dedicating projects, traveling long hours through the difficult terrain that is typical of rural Bolivia. They have been using two vehicles that were purchased with funds from the two foundations to travel up to nineteen hours daily for long distances. They wish for you to know the depth of their gratitude for vehicles that are safe, dependable, and comfortable. It would be impossible for them to serve many of the very needy isolated rural communities in which they work without this transportation.*

*They undertook a three-day trip, visiting four departments (states) of Bolivia, passing through many communities, sometimes with guides; sometimes following road signs and detours; sometimes arriving at midnight in a small community and awakening the neighbors so they could ask them if they were traveling on the correct road. They completed inspections for several new projects, the supervision of projects under construction, and selected sites for projects to which they had made commitments. In all, they traveled 1,900 kilometers (1,200 miles) over dreadful roads in three days! Then they traveled again last Saturday and Sunday to attend the dedications of two clinics in Potosí, using seldom-traveled roads. They also visited the Salar of Uyuni to evaluate a request. They used the vehicles again for this 1,400 kilometer (almost 900-mile) trip over dangerous, narrow, mountainous dirt roads.*

Lack of infrastructure not only results in endless days of travel, often on treacherous roads, it also creates unrelenting difficulties that are hard for outsiders to imagine. Rural Bolivia offers no telephones and no mail delivery, only dreadful roads. One cannot simply call or write to arrange a meeting, communicate an urgent request, take a photo for a newsletter, or just get something done. As a consequence, the majority of international nonprofits that work in Bolivia choose to focus on urban or peri-urban communities. Mano a Mano's commitment to improve health and economic well-being in rural Bolivia has required the willingness to work through these hardships on a daily basis.

An MMNM staff member describes transporting equipment to a building site:

*When moving a bulldozer from one project site to another, we found that the road was often too narrow and the turns too sharp to accommodate the low-boy that carried it. Every few miles we had to unload the dozer, use it to widen or repair the road, and then drive it back onto the low-boy. We repeated this process countless times before reaching our destination. When the road became a narrow trail that could not accommodate the low-boy, we rented a local logging truck to transport the dozer the remaining fifteen miles. Only after completing this seven-day arduous journey could work on the actual project begin.*

## Focus on Frugality

Segundo and I share an ethic of frugality that permeates Mano a Mano. As a result, we have accomplished astonishing results with modest expenditures. We often wonder how other international aid organizations can have much larger budgets, but accomplish so much less. Having always made do with limited resources, our natural response is to think through needs before spending assets, in the most economical fashion possible. Our frugality has promoted organizational creativity and endurance.

However, an organization needs to balance the desire for frugality with the goal of building organizational capacity. Here is one illustration of the difficulties that can arise when funds must stretch too far or when the needs of one part of the organization are sacrificed for another's. The Bolivian staff and volunteers work long hours in very difficult conditions. The machine operators and master builders labor in punishing environments of high altitude, extreme cold, constant fog, and dust driven by wind, often spending weeks apart from their families in order to complete their projects. Initially, communities agreed to provide them with food and overnight accommodations because no restaurants or motels exist in these areas. However, the community residents themselves have meager resources and often are not able to offer sufficient food or appropriate lodging. After years of frugality and making do with what each community could offer, Mano a Mano is now allocating some funds to reduce the hardships construction workers endure. We send basic food products with employees who will spend weeks at a remote work site, and continue to experiment with tents and mobile overnight units in which workers can sleep. In addition, we use our aviation program to fly staff from distant communities into Cochabamba for a few days of relaxation with their families and then back to their work sites.

Difficulties created by an intense focus on frugality have also affected the U.S. organization. Prior to 2005, the U.S. office transferred ninety-nine percent of donated funds to Bolivia, not retaining funds to cover expenses in the United States. Initially, this level of frugality encouraged donors who like to see their funds spent directly on clinics, schools, and water projects. Such extreme frugality enabled Mano a Mano to establish an impressive track record.

The recent economic downturn vastly increased the effort required to raise funds. At the same time, the accounting and reporting requirements for nonprofits increased. Mano a Mano's U.S. office workload expanded exponentially. Yet we only had two full-time staff members plus Segundo and me, who continued to work full-time on a pro bono basis. Gradually, this serious issue is being addressed and the organization is moving toward a more solid footing in the United States. The U.S. office now receives funds that are dedicated to its Twin Cities' programs, and we are including these costs as a line item in all grant applications.

## Systemic Corruption in Bolivia

For decades, perhaps centuries, Bolivians have viewed their government as one in which officials divert the country's resources into their own pockets and respond only to those who offer bribes. Mano a Mano made two intentional decisions regarding corruption: under no circumstance would we offer a bribe to a public official, and no Mano a Mano funds would flow through any level of the Bolivian government.

Our Bolivian counterparts face corruption continually as they attempt to accomplish their work. Liberating cargo held up in customs and complying with legal requirements placed on nonprofit organizations present the temptation to bribe an official, in what might appear to be the most feasible and perhaps the only way to proceed.

Mano a Mano has consistently stood its ground and has become respected throughout Bolivia as an organization that does not tolerate corruption. During the dedication of projects, municipal officials and representatives of the Ministry of Health often praise Mano a Mano for this stance.

Mano a Mano refuses to allow funds to flow through any level of the Bolivian government, to avoid misuse of donor funds and to enforce our ethic of frugality. On one occasion, a mayor informed Mano a Mano that all funds for a proposed clinic project would have to flow through and be disbursed by his office. José in turn informed the mayor that Mano a Mano always manages the project funds. "The clinic will not be built if that is your requirement," he said. Under intense pressure from community residents, the mayor withdrew his requirement and the clinic was built.

## Overarching Lessons Learned

Here are our top ten overarching lessons. They capture the essence of the Mano a Mano experience and are never far from our minds.

*Accomplish the work through trusted relationships.* Mano a Mano emerged from personal relationships among people who trusted each other to be well-intentioned, honest, and competent. To achieve our capacity-building mission in Bolivia, Mano a Mano has worked entirely through Bolivians. In contrast, many U.S.-based international organizations create subsidiary offices in their host country and place others from the United States in top positions there. Mano a Mano could not have achieved our successes without depending heavily on trusted individuals who have dedicated their lives to Mano a Mano and its programs. We note, however, that we learned through painful experience the advisability of "putting it in writing."

*Draw constantly on a bicultural perspective.* Every cross-cultural interaction and task carries the potential for the creative development of ideas and for hurtful misunderstandings. A deep understanding of both U.S. and Bolivian perspectives has made it possible for Mano a Mano to avoid or correct cultural missteps and continue with our mission.

*Begin small.* By starting on a small scale, Mano a Mano was able to resolve issues that would have been insurmountable had the organization been overwhelmed with too much too soon. If we had begun with a donation of 50,000 pounds of medical surplus, we would not have been able to manage it while resolving issues related to transporting it to Bolivia or clearing customs. Similarly, with each program area, pilot projects provided an opportunity to refine the model, the processes, and the product to enable an effective scale-up. "Begin small" applies equally to organizational structure. Any formal organizational structure must begin with definition of the mission, validation of its concept, and clear thinking about program development.

*Be systematic.* Mano a Mano attempted to think through each new process from beginning to end as a strategy to avoid potential problems; to launch every new project with a modest pilot; and to position the organization to take advantage of opportunities. We were always guided by a consistent framework of principles and values.

*Use the special skills and talents of the organization's founders.* Initially Mano a Mano focused on collecting and distributing medical supplies. At that time, Segundo and I had no other plan in mind. As we experienced success, we began to consider other needs to which we might respond and recognized that, in an organization comprised entirely of volunteers, we would have to assume responsibility for any expansion to additional projects because there was no funding for salaries.

Mano a Mano did not attempt to develop programs in areas in which we could not count on uncompensated expertise, such as establishing libraries or initiating a microloan program.

*Stay close and focus on beneficiaries.* A relatively flat organization with frequent beneficiary contact enables staff to stay close to those they serve. Mano a Mano created Bolivian counterpart NGOs to help maintain close contact and to ensure planning from the ground up. Experience has demonstrated how important it is for funders and volunteers to maintain frequent communication regarding beneficiary needs and project outcomes. In-country visits have been a powerful way to build strong connections.

*Ensure that projects belong to the community.* Materially poor rural communities request project partnerships with Mano a Mano. Projects remain community-driven with residents taking responsibility for long-term management. The fact that no Mano a Mano project has failed to function as intended speaks to the power of this approach.

*Present a clear message.* Mano a Mano began with a simple, straightforward message: We will collect the usable medical surplus that you discard and use it to make the difference between life and death. With each expansion, the organization worked on presenting a brief and compelling message.

*Nurture donors and keep them informed.* Donors want to know that their gifts improve lives and that donated funds are spent carefully. Mano a Mano responds to almost every donation within a week of receiving it, ensures that foundations receive complete and accurate reports, and e-mails frequent albeit brief stories about our projects to each donor.

*Focus on sustainable results.* Sustaining projects over the long term becomes a serious challenge for any nonprofit organization unless it is willing and able to manage the projects far into the future. To address this issue, Mano a Mano searched for a means of sustaining projects so we could move on to assist additional communities. We decided that the only feasible approach would be to establish partnerships with communities and their municipal officials. Legal partnership agreements formalize roles and responsibilities. These agreements require that municipalities take responsibility for maintaining the projects, thus fostering their long-term viability. We credit this model with our success. As more of Bolivia's national government resources are allocated to rural areas, municipalities can contribute more funding to joint projects. These partnerships vastly increase the number of projects we can undertake and, accordingly, benefit increasing numbers of rural residents. Mano a Mano also encourages each of our counterpart organizations to seek opportunities to use equipment and resources to raise funds and work toward self-sufficiency (as is the case with our aviation program).

◆ ◆ ◆ ◆

## Looking Back, Looking Ahead

Our dreams were unpretentious. We wanted to help. We wanted to make a difference in someone's life. We wanted to share our abundance with others. We couldn't abide waste. We were intrigued by the idea that medical supplies quite sensibly deemed useless by the medical establishment here might be put to use elsewhere. Whatever we did, however small, we were convinced that it might matter to someone 4,000 miles away.

As the years went by, we gained confidence and sophistication. We learned to dream more expansively. We learned to count miles and bricks. We learned to track our accomplishments.

We wanted to make a lasting difference. What counts? A brick clinic will stand for decades. A brick-and-mortar school building will last for generations. The structures themselves change the landscape, but they can also do much more.

The medical and educational systems we've helped put in place, we are convinced, change how the rural villagers think about themselves, their communities, and their children's futures. Little by little, we believe, they will come to think of available health care as essential and schools as indispensable. In this way, too, Mano a Mano will have made another kind of lasting imprint.

Looking ahead, we hope the Mano a Mano model of community participation will be more widely adopted by other NGOs. We like to think it will enjoy similar success with deserving populations in other corners of the world.

# Notes

1  Emerson, Ralph Waldo. "Fate." The Conduct of Life. Boston: Ticknor & Fields, 1860.

2  Matt Burgess. "World's Largest Protected Wetland Area Established in Bolivia," Positive News. London & Wales: Positive News Publishing, Ltd., 11 March 2013. Retrieved November 29, 2013: <http://www.positivenews.org.uk/2013/environment/ 11349/worlds>.

3  James J. Parsons. "Amazon River," Encyclopaedia Britannica Online. Encyclopaedia Britannica, Inc., 2013. Retrieved November 30, 2013: <http://www.britannica.com/EBchecked/topic/18707/Amazon-Rainforest>.

4  Rex A. Hudson and Dennis M. Hanratty, eds. "The Economy." Bolivia: A Country Study. 3rd ed. Washington, D.C.: Federal Research Division, Library of Congress, 1991. 138–42.

5  Guinness World Records. (2014) New York: Jim Pattison Group. Retrieved December 1, 2013: <http://www.guinnessworldrecords.com/records-12000/ highest-commercially-navigable-lake>.

6  "Bolivia." (2013) National Geographic. Retrieved November 30, 2013: <http://travel.nationalgeographic.com/travel/countries/bolivia-facts/>.

7  Denis Lepage. (2013) "Checklist of Birds of Bolivia," Bird Checklists of the World. Retrieved November 30, 2013: <http://avibase.bsc-eoc.org/checklist.jsp?lang=EN>.

8  Hudson and Hanratty.

9  "Bolivia." The World Book Encyclopedia, vol. B-2. Chicago: World Book, 2013.

10 Charles W. Arnade. "Bolivia: Languages and Religion," Encyclopaedia Britannica Online. Encyclopaedia Britannica, 2013. Retrieved November 30, 2013: <http://www.britannica.com/EBchecked/topic/72106/Bolivia>.

11   Charles W. Arnade. "War of the Pacific," Encyclopaedia Britannica Online. Encyclopaedia Britannica, 2013. Retrieved December 3, 2013: <http://www.britannica.com/EBchecked/topic/72106/Bolivia>.

12   "Poorest Countries in South America." (2013). Montreal: Aneki.com. Retrieved November 30, 2013: <http://www.aneki.com/poorest_south_america.html>.

13   Global Poverty Working Group, "Poverty Headcount Ratio at National Poverty Line" (% of Population—2009). World Development Indicators, 2013. Retrieved December 1, 2013: <http://data.worldbank.org/indicator/SI.POV.NAHC>.

14   Massimilano Cali and Juis Carlos Jemio, "Progress on Reaching the MDGs in Bolivia, p. 3, Fig. 1." Bolivia: Case Study for the MDG Gap Task Force Report. May 2010. Retrieved December 1, 2013: <http://www.un.org/en/development/desa/policy/mdg_gap/mdg_gap2010/mdggap_bolivia_case-study.pdf>.

15   Global Poverty Working Group, "Poverty Headcount Ratio at Urban Poverty Line." (2013). World Development Indicators, 2013. Retrieved December 1, 2013: <http://data.worldbank.org/topic/agriculture-and-rural-development>.

16   World Bank, "Bolivia: Rural population (% of total population)." (2012). Retrieved February 11, 2014: <http://www.quandl.com/WORLDBANK/BOL_SP_RUR_TOTL_ZS-Bolivia-Rural-population-of-total-population>.

17   Global Poverty Working Group, "Poverty Headcount Ratio at Rural Poverty Line." (2013) World Development Indicators, 2013. Retrieved December 1, 2013: <http://data.worldbank.org/indicator/SI.POV.RUHC>.

18   Arnade. "War of the Pacific."

19   World Food Programme, "Bolivia." < http://www.wfp.org/countries/bolivia/overview>.

20  Miguel Barrientos and Claudia Soria, "Bolivia—Life Expectancy at Birth," Index Mundi (source: UN Statistical Div., Population & Vital Statistics Report). Retrieved November 30, 2013: < http://www.indexmundi.com/facts/ Bolivia/life-expectancy-at-birth>.

21  Erika Silva and Ricardo Batisto, "Bolivian Maternal Child Health Policies: Successes and Failures." Canadian Foundation for the Americas Policy Paper, May 2010.

22  "Health Situation in the Americas: Basic Indicators, 2013." Pan American Health Organization. Retrieved December 2, 2013: <http://new.paho.org/ hq/dmdocuments>.

23  "Health Situation in the Americas."

24  Silva and Batisto, "Bolivian Maternal Child Health Policies."

25  Ibid.

26  Thomas Brinkhoff, "Literacy Rates—World by Map." Global Poverty Working Group. World Development Indicators, 2013. Retrieved December 1, 2013: <http://databank.worldbank.org/data/download/WDI-2013-eb-ook.pdf>.

27  Luke Metcalfe, "Bolivian Education Statistics." Retrieved December 1, 2013: <http://www.NationMaster.com/country/bl-bolivia/edu-education>.

28  Marcelo Cabrelo and Marcel Szekely, eds. *Educacion para la transformacion*. Banco de Desarollo Interamericano, 2012. Retrieved February 4, 2014. http://idbdocs.iadb.org/wsdocs/getDocument.aspx?DOCNUM=37259235

29  Ibid., 18.

30  Charles W. Arnade, "Bolivia: Education, Health, and Welfare," Encyclopaedia Britannica Online. Encyclopaedia Britannica, 2013. Retrieved November 30, 2013: <http://www.britannica.com/EBchecked/topic/ 72106/Bolivia>.

31  Paul Arnsberger, Melissa Ludlum, Margaret Riley, and Mark Stanton, "A History of the Tax-Exempt Sector: An SOI Perspective." Statistics of Income Bulletin, Winter 2008. Retrieved December 1, 2013: <http://www.irs.gov/pub/irs-soi/tehistory.pdf>.

32  Lindsay P. Galway, Kitty K. Corbett, and Leilei Zeng, "Where Are the NGOs and Why? The Distribution of Health and Development NGOs in Bolivia." BioMed Central, Ltd., November 23, 2012. Retrieved December 1, 2013: <http://www.globalizationandhealth.com/content/8/1/38>.

33  Ibid.

34  Ibid.

35  Ibid.

36  "Rescue Efforts Continue after Bolivian Quake." CNN World News, May 22, 1998. Retrieved December 1, 2013: <http://www.cnn.com/WORLD/americas/98051/22 bolivia.earthquake>.

37  Global Poverty Working Group, "Roads, Total Network." World Development Indicators, 2013. Retrieved December 1, 2013: <http://www.data.worldbank.org/data-catalog/world-development-indicators>.

38  Global Poverty Working Group, "Roads, Paved (% of Total Roads—2010)." World Development Indicators, 2013. Retrieved December 1, 2013: <http://www.data. worldbank.org/data-catalog/world-development-indicators>.

39  William Carter, "The Divided Society." Bolivia: a Profile. New York: Praeger Publishers, 1971. 81–105.

40  Joshua Partlow, "U.S. Trade Move Shakes Bolivia." The Washington Post, October 19, 2008. Retrieved December 2, 2013: <http://www.washingtonpost.com/wp-dyn/content/article/2008/10/18/>.

41 Jeremy McDermott, "Bolivia Expels U.S. Ambassador Philip Goldberg." The Telegraph, September 12, 2008. Retrieved December 2, 2013: <http://www.telegraph.co.uk/news/worldnews/southamerica/bolivia>.

42 "Last of DEA's Agents in Bolivia Leave Country." The Washington Post, January 30, 2009. Retrieved December 2, 2013: < http://www.washington-post.com/wp-dyn/content/article/2009/01/29/AR2009012903735.html>.

43 "Bolivia and U.S. to Restore Ties." The New York Times, November 7, 2011. Retrieved December 2, 2013: <http://www.nytimes.com/2011/11/08/world/americas/bolivia-and-united-states-to-restore-ties.html?_r=0>.

44 William Neuman, "U.S. Agency is Expelled from Bolivia." The New York Times, U.S. Edition, May 1, 2013. Retrieved December 2, 2013: <http://www.nytimes. com/.../bolivian-president-expels-us-aid-agency/html>.

45 U.S. Department of State, Bureau of Economic and Business Affairs, "2012 Investment Climate Statement," June 2012. Retrieved December 2, 2013: <http://www.state.gov/e/eb/rls/othr/ics/2012/191112.htm>.

46 Sofia Wickburg, U4 Anti-Corruption Resource Center, "Bolivia: Overview of Corruption and Anti-Corruption." U4 Expert Answer, No. 346, 27 September 2012. Retrieved December 2, 2013: <http://www.u4.no/publications/bolivia-overview-of-corruption-and-anti-corruption/>.

47 Department of Legal Cooperation, Organization of American States, "Bolivia Adopts Anti-Corruption Law." Anti-Corruption, Edition N-35, July 2010. Retrieved December 2, 2013: <http://www.oas.org/juridico/newsletter/nl_en_35.htm>.

48 Saul Alinsky. Reveille for Radicals. New York: Vintage Books, 1989. 54.

49 National Association of Social Workers, "Code of Ethics," approved by the 1996 NASW Delegate Assembly and revised by the 2008 NASW Delegate Assembly. Retrieved December 2, 2013: <http://www.socialworkers.org/pubs/code/ code.asp>.

50  International Federation of Social Workers, "Statement of Ethical Principles," March 3, 2012. Retrieved December 2, 2013: <http://www.ifsw.org/policies/statement-of-ethical-principles>.

51  Joan Velásquez, Marilyn E. Vigil, and Eustolio Benavides, "A Framework for Establishing Social Work Relationships Across Racial/Ethnic Lines." Social Work Processes. Ed. Compton, Beulah, Burt Galaway, and Barry R. Cournoyer. Belmont, California: Dorsey Press, 1979. 239.

52  Margaret Mead, "The Institute for Intercultural Studies." Trademark held by Sevanne Kassarjian, New York. Used with permission. Retrieved December 2, 2013: <http://www.interculturalstudies.org/faq.html>.

53  Amartya Sen. Development of Freedom. New York: Alfred A. Knopf, 1999.

54  Galway, Corbett, and Zeng, "Where Are the NGOs?"

55  Kingsolver, Barbara, "Water is Life." National Geographic, April 2010. Retrieved December 2, 2013. <http://ngm.nationalgeographic.com/2010/04/water-is-life/kingsolver-text>.

56  Samantha Carter, interview at Mano a Mano US office, August 17, 2013.

57  David Hanna. Designing Organizations for High Performance. New York: Addison-Wesley Publishing Co., 1988. 38.

58  Michael Q. Patton, "Evaluation for the Way We Live." Developmental Evaluation: Applying Complexity Concepts to Enhance Innovation and Use. New York: The Guilford Press, 2006.

# Acknowledgments

Everything that Mano a Mano does is a collaborative, group effort; thank you to those who have worked hand in hand together—mano a mano—to "make history in Bolivia." Without you, there would have been nothing to write about!

- Mano a Mano staff in the U.S. and Bolivia whose devotion to creating a more just world gives them the *ganas* to persevere and to excel at this work;

- Volunteers in the U.S. and Bolivia and from across the globe who have recognized the significance of this work and contributed countless unpaid hours to making it happen;

- Our donors—foundations, corporations, small businesses, civic groups, churches, and hundreds of individuals—who believed in our vision and had confidence in us to be good stewards of their gifts;

- The rural Bolivian community leaders and municipal officials who became true partners on our projects;

- The thousands of Bolivian community volunteers whose hard manual labor brought these projects into being and will ensure that they are sustained;

- The Bolivian Ministry of Health and Sports for recognizing the importance of our community clinic program and funding most of its staff over the long term.

Thank you to our anonymous donor. Your funding served as the major building block in the expansion of our clinic program, which has made health care accessible to hundreds of thousands. And thank you to Reverend John Slettom for initiating and nurturing this crucial connection.

This book has grown organically, much as Mano a Mano has done. Thanks to the dozens who offered advice, edited, photographed, and created graphs throughout its many iterations. And a special thanks to:

- Nate Knatterud–Hubinger, Mano a Mano's Director of Communications and Research, whose in-depth grasp of our approach to development helped shaped the content and focus of this writing and move it from years-worth of notes to a book;

- Kitty Gogins for pushing us to move forward with this project and outlining it;

- Christine Ver Ploeg, devoted member of our U.S. board, for her introduction, always-available consultation, innumerable reviews, and extensive editing;

- Judith Picken, dear friend and formidable writer, for transforming the sentence structure from beginning to end, making it flow, and asking all the right questions.

And, finally, to all members of the Velásquez family who have shared the vision for this work and contributed endless hours and their expertise to improving life in Bolivia's rural communities.

# Foundation Contributors

Alternative Gifts International
Anonymous Donor Foundation
Caterpillar Foundation
Chiron Foundation
The Conservation, Food & Health Foundation
Dunn Associates
Edwin W. and Catherine M. Davis Foundation
Eliot Street Fund
Foundation for the Development of Human Potential
Geneva Global
Graziano Medin Family Foundation
Innovations, Inc./Prepare and Enrich
Irwin Andrew Porter Foundation
Izumi Foundation
James Dougherty Jr. Foundation
John P. and Eleanor R. Yackel Foundation
Joseph A. and Charlotte K. Blitt Charitable Fund
Laura Jane Musser Fund
Lennox Foundation
Lored Foundation
May and Stanley Smith Charitable Trust
Mendon F. Schutt Family Fund
New England Biolabs Foundation
Northwest Airlines AirCares Community Support Program
Open Road Alliance
Opus Prize Foundation
Pentair Foundation
RJN Foundation
Rotary Foundation
Sundance Family Foundation
The Athwin Foundation
The Brent Family Foundation
The ERM Group Foundation

The International Foundation
The Medtronic Foundation
The West Foundation
Wagner Foundation, Ltd.
Wagner-Essman CARE Foundation, Inc.
Weyerhaeuser Family Foundation
Women's Foundation of Minnesota

## Rotary Contributors

Brooklyn Park Rotary
Crystal-New Hope-Robbinsdale Rotary
Downtown Duluth Rotary
Duluth Skyline Rotary
Fargo West Rotary
FM/AM Rotary – Fargo
Harbortown Rotary – Duluth
Minnetonka Rotary
Moorhead Rotary
Pine City Rotary
Rotary Club 25 of Duluth
Rotary Club of Saint Paul
Rotary International
Superior Wisconsin Rotary
Vadnais Heights Rotary